MASTERING THE TAKS GRADE 4 IN READING AND WRITING

JAMES KILLORAN

STUART ZIMMER

MARK JARRETT

JARRETT PUBLISHING COMPANY

East Coast Office
P.O. Box 1460
19 Cross Street
Ronkonkoma, NY 11779
631-981-4248

West Coast Office
10 Folin Lane
Lafayette, CA 94549
925-906-9742

1-800-859-7679   Fax: 631-588-4722
www.jarrettpub.com

This book includes material from many different sources. Occasionally it is not possible to determine if a particular source is copyrighted, and if so, who is the copyright owner. Every effort has been made to trace the ownership of all copyrighted material and to secure the necessary permissions to reprint these selections. If there has been a copyright infringement with any material in this book, it is unintentional. We extend our sincerest apologies and would be happy to make immediate and appropriate restitution upon proof of copyright ownership.

Grateful acknowledgment is made to the following to reprint the copyrighted materials listed below:

Black Dog and Leventhal Publishers for "Alvin Ailey" by Andrea Davis Pinkney in *African-American Read Aloud Stories,* © 1998. Reprinted with permission of Johnny D. Boggs and *Boys' Life,* for "Along the Herd Highway," February 1999 issue, published by the Boy Scouts of America. Children's Better Health Institute for the articles in *Child Life,* "Happy Birthday, Basketball" by Charles Davis in the March 2000 issue; *Elizabeth Blackwell: The First Woman Doctor* in the April/May 2000 issue, from *Health Explorer,* © 1981 by Children's Better Health Institute, Benjamin Franklin Literary and Medical Society, Inc., Indianapolis, Indiana. Used by permission. *Cobblestone Magazine* for the article, "School Days" by Joyce Haynes in the February 1999 issue. *Cricket Magazine* for the story, "Killer" by Sandy Fox in the August 1998 issue; for the article, "When Money Grew on Trees" by Amy Butler Greenfield in the August 2001 issue. *Highlights for Children* for the story, "Abby Takes Her Shot" by Susan Dyckman in the January 2001 issue; for the story, "The Recital" by Kathleen Bennere Duble, in the February 1999 issue; for the story, "The Mystery of the Unfriendly Neighbor" by Diane Burns in the September, 2001 issue. Pleasant Company Publications for the novel *Josefina Learns a Lesson* by Valerie Tripp, © 1997. Simon and Schuster for the story "The Emperor and the Peasant Boy," in *The Book of Virtues for Young People,* edited by William J. Bennett, © 1997. *Spider: The Magazine for Children* for: "Hard-Boiled Eggs" a tale from Hungary retold by Tom R. Kovach, in the March, 2003 issue. "The Lion's Whisker" excerpted from *Thirty-Three Multi-cultural Tales to Tell,* © 1993 by Pleasant L. DeSpain; used by permission of August House Publishers. ***NOTE:*** *In some cases, previously published material has been edited to maintain a fourth-grade readability level.*

Copyright 2003 by Jarrett Publishing Company

All rights reserved. No part of this book may be reproduced in any form or by any means, including electronic, photographic, mechanical, or by any device for storage and retrieval of information, without the express written permission of the publisher. Requests for permission to copy any part of this book should be mailed to:

Jarrett Publishing Company
Post Office Box 1460
19 Cross Street
Ronkonkoma, New York 11779

ISBN 1-882422-75-9
Printed in the United States of America
by Malloy, Inc., Ann Arbor, Michigan
First Edition
10 9 8 7 6 5 4 3 2 1   06 05 04 03

ACKNOWLEDGMENTS

The authors would like to thank the following Texas educator who helped review the manuscript. Her comments, suggestions, and recommendations have proved invaluable in preparing this book.

Deborah Havens Ph.D.
Director, Special Services
Formerly with the Texas Education Agency
and U.S. Department of Education
Austin Area Charter School Cooperative
Austin, Texas

Cover design, layout, graphics, and typesetting: Burmar Technical Corporation, Albertson, N.Y. The authors would also like to thank Julia and Alex Jarrett for samples of fourth-grade writing.

This book is dedicated…

to my wife Donna, my children Christian, Carrie, and Jesse, and
my grandson Aiden — *James Killoran*

to my wife Joan, my children Todd and Ronald, and
my grandchildren Jared and Katie — *Stuart Zimmer*

to my wife Gośka, and my children Alexander and Julia — *Mark Jarrett*

Other books by Killoran, Zimmer, and Jarrett

Mastering the TAKS Grade 11 Exit Level ELA
Mastering the TAKS Grade 3 in Reading
Mastering the Grade 7 Writing TEKS
Mastering the Georgia Middle Grades Writing Assessment
Mastering the Grade 6 PSSA Writing Assessment
Mastering the Grade 5 PSSA Reading Test
Mastering the Grade 3 ISAT Reading and Writing Test
Mastering the Grade 5 ISAT Reading and Writing Test
Mastering the Grade 3 MCAS Reading Test
Mastering the Grade 4 MCAS Tests in English Language Arts
Mastering New York's Grade 4 English Language Arts Test
Mastering New York's Grade 8 English Language Arts Test
Mastering Ohio's Fourth Grade Proficiency Tests in Reading and Writing
Mastering the Grade 4 FCAT Reading and Writing Test
Introducing the Elementary English Language Arts
Mastering the Elementary English Language Arts

TABLE OF CONTENTS
PART 1: READING

Unit 1: Introduction
- **CHAPTER 1: HOW TO BE A GOOD READER** 2
- **CHAPTER 2: TYPES OF READINGS** 9

Unit 2: Preparing For The TAKS Grade 4 in Reading
- **CHAPTER 3: A PRACTICE PRETEST** 22
- **CHAPTER 4: WORD-MEANING QUESTIONS** 40
- **CHAPTER 5: QUESTIONS ON YOUR BASIC UNDERSTANDING OF A READING** 53
- **CHAPTER 6: QUESTIONS ON THE ELEMENTS OF A STORY** 68
- **CHAPTER 7: UNDERSTANDING HOW A READING WORKS** 84
- **CHAPTER 8: GOING BEYOND THE READING** 97
- **CHAPTER 9: QUESTIONS ABOUT PAIRED READINGS** 108

Unit 3: A Practice Reading Test
- **CHAPTER 10: A PRACTICE TAKS GRADE 4 IN READING** 116

PART 2: WRITING

Unit 4: The Written Composition
- **CHAPTER 11: FOCUS AND COHERENCE** 132
- **CHAPTER 12: THE DEVELOPMENT OF IDEAS** 141
- **CHAPTER 13: ORGANIZATION** 147
- **CHAPTER 14: VOICE** 155
- **CHAPTER 15: THE WRITING PROCESS** 160
- **CHAPTER 16: WRITING FOR DIFFERENT PURPOSES** 169

Unit 5: Peer Editing
- **CHAPTER 17: ORGANIZATION AND SENTENCE CONSTRUCTION** 181
- **CHAPTER 18: USAGE** 189
- **CHAPTER 19: MECHANICS** 198

Unit 6: A Practice Writing Test
- **CHAPTER 20: A PRACTICE TAKS GRADE 4 IN WRITING** 204

UNIT 1: INTRODUCTION

 Chapter 1: How to Be a Good Reader

 Chapter 2: Types of Readings

This year you will take two important tests — the **TAKS Grade 4 in Reading** and the **TAKS Grade 4 in Writing.** This book will help you prepare for both tests, as well as show you how to improve your reading and writing skills. The **TAKS Grade 4 in Reading** will test your ability to read and answer questions about stories and informational selections. This first unit introduces you to certain skills that will help you to become a better reader:

★ In the first chapter you will learn what good readers do to understand what they have read.

★ There are several types of selections you should be able to read in fourth grade. Chapter 2 looks at stories, including their setting, characters, and plot. This chapter also looks at informational readings, such as a magazine article. These provide information on a topic.

CHAPTER 1

HOW TO BE A GOOD READER

Would you like to be a better reader? Recognizing words is just part of being a good reader. The most important part of reading is **understanding** the ideas of the writer and seeing how these fit in with your own ideas.

A good reader is an **active** reader. When you read, be sure to ask yourself questions. Think about how the author's ideas match up with your own. Thinking about what you read helps you to understand the reading better. In this chapter, you will learn some important ways of thinking about what you read. These include things you should think about *before, during,* and *after* you read any selection.

BEFORE READING

When you are about to read something, you should always ask yourself:

- Why am I reading this selection?
- What do I already know about this subject?

Think about *why* you are reading the selection. For example, is it to find out information or to enjoy a good story?

Next, look over the title and the rest of the selection to get some general idea of what the reading is about. See if there are illustrations, headings, or other clues about the subject of the reading. Then think about what you already know about this kind of reading and its subject. Finally, ask yourself what would you like to find out about that topic.

DURING READING

Good readers actively think while they read. You can do this by using the following methods:

Make Connections. Connect the reading to what you already know. As you read, ask yourself if each new thing you read about reminds you of anything you already know. This could be something that happened to you or that you read or heard about. Compare the reading to what you already know.

Ask Questions. As you read, ask yourself questions. For example, ask *where* and *when* the action takes place. Good readers ask *what* is happening in the reading. They also ask *why* things in the story happen the way they do. Asking yourself questions helps you to stay focused on what you are reading.

Think about What Is Important. As you read, focus on the author's *main ideas* or the *key events* in the story. Ask yourself which details are important for understanding what the author has to say. The title is important because it often tells you what the selection is about. Many paragraphs will have **topic sentences** stating the main idea of the paragraph.

Make Mental Pictures. Much of what we know about the world comes through our five senses. When you read, try to picture the things you are reading about. Imagine what it would be like to see, smell, taste, or touch what a character is experiencing.

Make Predictions. As you read, try to predict what will happen next. For example, if a character in a story faces a problem, think about some ways the problem could be solved. Then see if the character solved the problem using one of the ways you thought of.

 Summarize. When you read, you should pause sometimes to think about what you have just read. Silently summarize what is important in your own words. Check any details you are not sure about before you read on.

 Be a Problem-Solver. If you have trouble understanding something, don't just continue reading. Take steps to figure it out. For example, re-read a difficult section to understand it better. Try to figure out the meaning of a difficult word by looking at surrounding words and sentences, or look it up in a dictionary.

The following chart summarizes the methods used by good readers. See how many of these methods you can use when you read.

STRATEGIES USED BY GOOD READERS

Make Connections
Good readers make connections with what they already know as they read.

Ask Questions
Good readers ask themselves questions as they read a passage.

Think about What's Important
Good readers think about what is important as they read.

Create Mental Images
Good readers make mental images as they read. They picture what is happening in the story or text.

Make Predictions
Good readers make predictions and draw conclusions as they read.

Summarize
Good readers summarize the text in their own words as they read.

Be a Problem-Solver
When good readers cannot understand something, they take special steps to figure it out.

AFTER READING

After you finish reading a selection, think about what you have just read. Think again about what was **most important** in the reading. Mentally **summarize** what the reading was about. Think about what you learned from the reading and how it fits in with what you know. Ask yourself the following:

★ What was the message or main idea of the reading?

★ Have I learned anything *new*?

★ What were some "memorable" words and phrases?

PRACTICE MODEL

Let's see how a good reader actually uses these methods. On the following page is a sample reading selection about the Native Americans of the Great Lakes. This model shows what a good reader thinks about *before, during,* and *after* reading.

BEFORE READING

Before reading, a good reader asks:

> ★ *Why am I reading this?*
> I am reading this selection to find out about the Native American tribes who once lived around the Great Lakes.
>
> ★ *What do I already know about this subject?*
> I have studied the Native American tribes of Texas in school. I do not know anything about Native American tribes living as far north as the Great Lakes. However, I know the Great Lakes are large freshwater lakes in the northern part of the United States.

DURING READING

Here are some things a good reader might think about while reading this article:

The Junior Encyclopedia

Native American Tribes of the Great Lakes

The Great Lakes are five of the largest freshwater lakes in the world. They are located between the United States and Canada. Long before the voyages of Christopher Columbus, Native American tribes lived along the shores of the Great Lakes. Members of these tribes developed ways of life that used the resources nature made available to them.

MAKE CONNECTIONS
I know about freshwater lakes. This information helps me make connections with this kind of environment.

MAKE PREDICTIONS
From the text, I can tell this is an article, not a story. I predict the article will tell me facts about the lifestyles of the Great Lakes tribes.

CREATE MENTAL IMAGES
I can just imagine how the Native American settlements looked, scattered in the forests around the Great Lakes.

What other connections can you make from the title?
_____
_____
_____

What other predictions would you make?
_____
_____
_____

What other mental pictures would you create?
_____
_____
_____

CHAPTER 1: HOW TO BE A GOOD READER

Most of the villages of the Great Lakes tribes were built near rivers or lakes. Canoes were used for transportation and to search for food. Usually, the men did the hunting, fishing, and making of canoes. They used natural materials, such as rocks and plant fibers, to make tools and weapons. They used spears, hooks, and nets to fish in the Great Lakes. Bows and arrows, spears and clubs were used to kill deer, rabbits, moose, squirrels, beavers, ducks, and turkeys. Some meat and fish were preserved for later use in the winter.

ASK QUESTIONS
As I read, I ask myself the following questions:
- ❏ How many people lived in a typical village?
- ❏ What did their homes look like?
- ❏ How did they make their canoes?
- ❏ What kinds of fish did they catch?

What other questions would you ask?

_____

_____

Women gathered berries, nuts and other wild plants. Children helped gather berries and wild rice. Women were also in charge of growing corn, squash, beans, potatoes and other vegetables. Corn was a major food in their diet. Women crushed corn in stone bowls to make the flour used in breads or stews.

THINK ABOUT WHAT IS IMPORTANT
This paragraph seems important. It tells what things the women and children did, and what kinds of foods they grew.

What other information do you think is important in this article?

_____

_____

GOING BEYOND THE READING

After reading a selection, a good reader thinks about what he or she has learned. Here, the reader learned some things about the lifestyles of the Native American tribes living around the Great Lakes. After reading this article, the reader might:

★ add some new words — like *canoe, fibers* or *preserved* — to a list of vocabulary words;

★ search the Internet for more information about the Great Lakes tribes;

★ go to the library to take out books about other Native American tribes;

★ plan a family trip to visit the area around the Great Lakes; or

★ visit a Native American reservation.

CHAPTER 2

TYPES OF READINGS

There will be four types of selections on the **TAKS Grade 4 in Reading:** (1) stories, (2) informational readings, (3) mixed selections with features of each, and (4) paired readings. **Paired readings** are made up of two shorter selections on the same topic or theme.

STORIES

We read stories for enjoyment. Good stories can help us imagine what it would be like to live in faraway places or to enjoy exciting adventures. They teach us about other people's experiences and lives. Stories put us in touch with all kinds of emotions. They can make us laugh, cry, or make our hearts pound with excitement.

Every story has three main parts:

Do you know what each of these parts is? Let's look at a well-known story by Hans Christian Andersen to see how these parts work together.

THE EMPEROR'S NEW CLOTHES

1 Several hundred years ago a wealthy emperor lived in Europe who was quite fond of beautiful new clothes. He did not care about his soldiers or his people unless it was to show off his new clothes.

2 One day two thieves came to the town where the emperor's palace stood. The two thieves told everybody they were master tailors who could weave the most marvelous clothing. Not only were the colors and patterns of these clothes extraordinary, but the cloth had the strange quality of being invisible to anyone *unfit for his job* or *very stupid*.

3 "This is truly marvelous," the emperor thought when he heard of the master tailors. "Now if I had clothes cut from that material, I would know which of my counselors was unfit for his job. They must weave some material for me!" And he gave the thieves a large sum of money to start working without delay.

4 The thieves set up a loom and acted as if they were weaving. The fine gold threads they demanded from the emperor were never used. Each night they sat before their empty looms, pretending to weave.

5 "I would like to know if my new clothes are almost finished. I will send my Prime Minister to see the weavers," thought the emperor. "He will know how to judge the material, for he is both clever and fit for his job."

CONTINUED

6 The Prime Minister visited the weavers but saw an empty loom. He thought, "I can't see a thing! Am I stupid? I can't believe it. Maybe I am not fit for my job. I had better not admit I can't see what they're weaving."

7 "Tell us what you think," demanded the thieves. "It's beautiful. What patterns! What colors! I shall tell the emperor I'm greatly pleased," the Prime Minister answered. The two thieves now demanded even more money and greater quantities of gold thread. They said they needed it for weaving, but the loom remained as empty as ever.

8 Next, the emperor sent other ministers to see how the work was progressing. "Isn't it a marvelous piece of material?" asked the thieves as they described the beauty of the clothes to the ministers. "I'm not stupid," each minister repeated to himself, thinking he must be unfit for his job. Each one began to praise the loveliness of the clothing's patterns and colors.

9 At last the emperor decided to see the garment himself. With the most important people in his empire, he entered the room where the weavers were hard at work at their loom.

10 "I can't see a thing!" thought the emperor. "This is a disaster! Am I stupid? Am I not fit to be emperor?" But aloud he said, "The clothes are so very lovely. They have my approval."

11 The next day, the new clothes were ready for the emperor to wear in a parade. "Will Your Majesty please take off your clothes?" asked the thieves. "We shall help you put on your new clothes."

CONTINUED

12   The thieves lifted their arms as if they were holding something in their hands and said, "These are the trousers and this is the robe. They are as light as if they were made of spider webs! It will be as if Your Majesty had almost nothing on, but that is their special beauty." The emperor did as he was told. The thieves acted as if they were dressing him in the clothes they had made. Finally, the emperor stood in front of a mirror admiring the clothes he couldn't see.

13   The emperor left to walk in the parade. All the people of the town, who had lined the streets, shouted to the emperor that his new clothes were beautiful. "What a magnificent robe! How well the emperor's clothes fit!"

14   None of the townspeople was willing to admit that he or she did not see a thing; for if anyone did, then he was either stupid or unfit for the job he held.

15   And then ever so softly from the crowd, a little child cried out: "But the emperor doesn't have anything on!" "Listen to the little one," said the proud father. And the people began to whisper among each other and repeated what the child had said.

16   "He doesn't have anything on. There's a child who says that the emperor has nothing on!" At last, all the people began to shout, "He has nothing on!"

17   The emperor shivered, for he was certain that they were right; but he thought, "I must hold my head high and put up with it until the parade is over." And he walked even more proudly, while across town the two thieves made their escape.

Let's take a look at all three parts of a story — setting, character, and plot.

The Setting. The story setting is **when** and **where** the story takes place. A story may have more than one setting if events occur at different times and places. A story setting can take place in the past, present, or future, or even in an imaginary world where time hardly seems to exist. *The Emperor's New Clothes* takes place hundreds of years ago in an empire somewhere in Europe.

The Characters. The characters are who the story is about. Characters can be made-up people or real people, in a make-believe setting. Story characters may even be animals. Most stories have only one or two main characters. When reading a story, ask yourself the following questions about its characters:

★ What are their special qualities?
★ How do they act, think, and feel?
★ How do they change as the story develops?

CHECKING YOUR UNDERSTANDING

Complete the diagram below identifying the characters of the story.

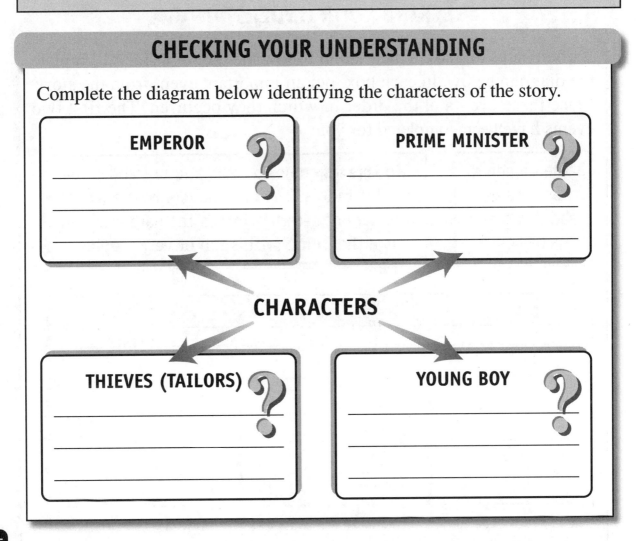

The Plot. In almost all stories, characters face one or more problems. For example, a character may want to do something that is difficult, or have a disagreement with another character in the story. The plot is what happens in the story. It is made up of the events of the story. As these events take place, the characters try to solve the main problem in the story.

When you read a story, ask yourself these questions about the plot:

★ What **problems** do the main characters face?
★ What **events** in the story affect these problems?
★ What **actions** do the characters take to deal with these problems?
★ How are these problems finally **resolved**?

CHECKING YOUR UNDERSTANDING

It often helps to make a diagram to follow the plot of a story. Complete the diagram below. In each box, put an important event from the story. Place these events in the order in which they occurred. The first two events have been completed for you:

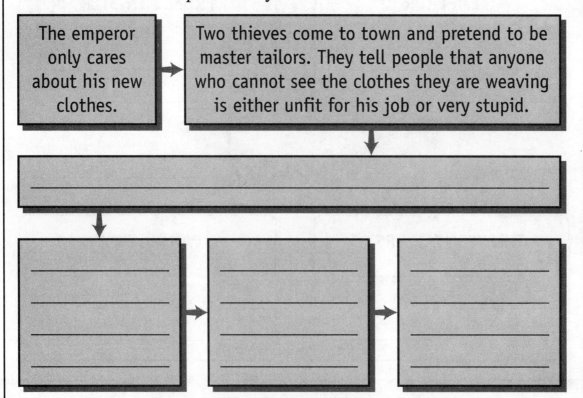

Another way to remember a story is by drawing pictures. Create a comic strip telling the main events of the story, *The Emperor's New Clothes*. Remember, it is *not* your art work that is important, but how well you show the story. Use a separate sheet of paper to create your comic strip.

READING FOR INFORMATION

A second type of reading selection you should be able to recognize is an informational reading, also known as *nonfiction*. **Informational readings** are about real people, places, events, and things. People read nonfiction to learn about things. A newspaper or magazine article is a type of informational reading. An article tells you the basic facts about something.

THE PARTS OF AN INFORMATIONAL READING

Just as stories have different parts, so do informational readings. There are *two* major parts to an informational reading:

To see how each part works, let's look at a short informational reading.

February 1999 — Vol. 7, Number 5

SCHOOL DAYS
by Joyce Haynes

In ancient Egypt, only the very smartest children went to school, where they learned to read and write. Most Egyptians never learned to read and write.

CONTINUED

The children who went to school learned to be scribes. Scribes were very important people in ancient Egypt because they were almost the only ones who could read and write. Although records tell us that there were a few female scribes, most were men. Boys entered scribal school when they were quite young and studied hard for about 10 to 12 years.

It took years to learn how to write the hundreds of signs called hieroglyphs. Ancient Egyptians used hieroglyphs to write their language. Just think, you only have to learn 26 letters!

Scribes also had to know how to write *hieratic*. This was a kind of shorthand script used for everyday writing. Students memorized the hieroglyphic signs and practiced writing them on pieces of stone, pottery, or wood. They practiced by copying all kinds of things that had already been written: letters, literature, religious records, and business and government documents. In this way, students learned more than just their language.

Hieroglyphics on the walls of the Temple of Amenophs III, around 1360 B.C.

Scribal students used writing tools somewhat like the parts of a water color set you might have. Ink was shaped into round disks, just like our paint sets. But instead of many colors, scribes used only red and black. The cakes of ink were made out of the mineral red ochre and out of black carbon from burnt sticks or pans. Scribes carried small pots of water to mix with the inks. Their brushes, made of reed plants, were held in a small case.

CONTINUED

Students often practiced writing on flat pieces of the limestone rock that could be found everywhere in Egypt. Many school texts, or homework, have been found on these flakes of stone. Sometimes a student or a scribe needed to write something very important. Then he wrote on papyrus paper, made from the reeds found along the Nile.

Tools used by Egyptian scribes — papyrus, ink palette, and a writing tool.

When a student finished scribe school, he could get a good job in ancient Egypt. He might become a doctor or a priest, the secretary to a noble family, the boss of a group of workers, or have some other job that required the ability to read and write.

The Egyptians wrote as many different kinds of things as we do. They wrote letters home and sent bills for work they had done. They wrote poetry and stories and put down words of wisdom and advice for their children. They wrote many prayers to their gods.

THE MAIN IDEA OF A READING

The **topic** or subject of an informational reading is what it is all about. In this example the topic of the reading is becoming a scribe in ancient Egypt. The general point that an author makes about the topic of a reading is known as the **main idea**.

MAIN IDEA

Ancient Egyptians studied very hard to become scribes.

FINDING THE MAIN IDEA

When you read for information, use two steps to find the main idea.

STEP 1: Determine the topic of the reading.

First, determine the general subject of the reading. What is it about? Is it about a person, place, event, or thing? Think of the topic as an umbrella. It should be large enough to cover everything discussed in the reading. In this selection about ancient Egypt, everything in the reading tells us about some aspect of being a scribe.

STEP 2: See what the writer is saying overall about the topic.

Once you have determined the topic, focus on what the writer has to say about it. Look for an overall message about the topic.

This message is the author's **main idea.** Other details in the reading should explain or support the main idea. In this reading, the main idea is that becoming a scribe was hard but important work. A scribe had to master hundreds of hieroglyphics and hieratic without many of the resources that we have today.

THE SUPPORTING DETAILS

To help the reader understand the main idea, a writer supplies examples, details, and illustrations. These are known as **supporting details.** They help to *support* the author's main idea. Through the use of these details, the author explains, illustrates, or proves the main idea of the reading.

CHAPTER 2: TYPES OF READINGS   19

CHECKING YOUR UNDERSTANDING

What details were used by the writer to support the idea that becoming a scribe in ancient Egypt was hard but worthwhile work? The first supporting detail has already been filled in for you.

★ An Egyptian had to study hard for ten to twelve years to become a scribe.

★

★

★

Use the illustration below to check your answers from the previous page.

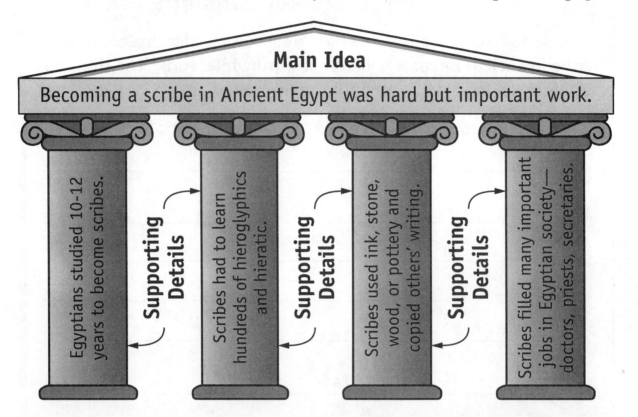

SUMMARY

In this chapter, you learned about two different types of readings.

IN A STORY

In a story, you can expect to find a <u>setting</u>, <u>characters</u>, and a <u>plot</u>.

IN AN INFORMATIONAL READING

In an informational reading, you can expect to find a <u>topic</u>, a <u>main idea</u> about that topic, and <u>supporting details</u>. Supporting details may include descriptions, facts, and examples.

UNIT 2: PREPARING FOR THE TAKS GRADE 4 IN READING

This year you will take the **TAKS Grade 4 in Reading.** In this unit, you will learn about the different types of questions on the test and how to answer them.

The first chapter in this unit is a practice test. This practice test will show you the types of readings and the kinds of questions found on the **TAKS Grade 4 in Reading.** You will also notice that after each question the word "objective" is followed by a number. This number refers to the type of skill the question is testing. This will allow your teacher to learn which objectives you and your classmates need the most help in mastering.

Later chapters in this unit will look at each type of question, such as *word-meaning questions,* what a paragraph or reading is "mostly about," or *summarizing questions.* You will learn how to answer each type of question and be given plenty of practice. In Unit 3, you will take another practice test. That test will show you how much you have improved.

CHAPTER 3

A PRACTICE PRETEST

This practice test has three reading selections. Like the actual **TAKS Grade 4 in Reading,** each selection is followed by a series of multiple-choice questions. Select the answer choice that best answers each question.

ABBY TAKES HER SHOT
By Susan M. Dyckman

1   A blast of the buzzer ended the game, and the Hawks had won another one. Abby leaped from the bench. Her throat hurt from cheering. The Hawks were undefeated after thirteen games — the best record a Willow Grove school team had ever had.

2   Not that Abby had made much of a contribution. Her playing time totaled only ten minutes for the entire season. It didn't help when her brother teased her. "You're a cheerleader in a basketball uniform," he said. "All you need are pom-poms."

3   Abby felt Mom's eyes on her from the bleachers. Abby forced a wave. At the meeting Coach McKenzie smiled. "Girls, your defense was awesome," she said. "And Kathy, your free-throw shooting helped a lot."

CONTINUED →

4 Abby felt like shouting, "My free-throw shooting could help, too — if I could just get in the game!" She thought of the hours she'd spent practicing. Mom said it was worth it. Abby was a fifth-grader, and she'd made the team. But Abby learned quickly that making the team and playing in games were two different things.

5 Mom was waiting in the car. Abby held back tears as she opened the door. "Are you OK?" Mom asked. Abby nodded. Mom squeezed her hand. Mom always knew when to say something.

6 Suppertime was quiet. Dad had taken her brother to a Scout meeting, so Abby was <u>spared</u> more teasing. After clearing the table, Abby went to her room to do homework. When she'd finished, Abby grabbed a basketball and raced downstairs. Mom came up behind her. "Want some company?" she asked.

7 "I guess," Abby answered. Mom took her spot under the basket. Abby always led off their games.

8 "I know what you're going to say," Abby began. "I made the team and I should be happy."

9 "Not this time," Mom said. She passed the ball back, and Abby hit a jump shot. "I'm so proud of you for hanging in there."

10 She held the ball tightly and looked at Mom. "I really thought I'd play more."

11 "I know you did, honey." Mom put her arms around Abby and hugged her. "Your time will come."

12 The gym was packed for the last game of the season. The lead seesawed back and forth, and the Hawks' starters were breathing hard at halftime. Coach McKenzie was encouraging. "Stick to your game," she said. "Don't shoot until you get an open shot."

13 Abby watched as the second half began. She watched as the players ran up and down the court. The score remained close, and the Hawks trailed by one point in the final minute.

14 "Come on, Hawks," Abby shouted.

15 A few seconds later, Kathy stole the ball and raced toward the basket. As she went up for the shot, an opponent slammed into her, knocking her to the floor. Kathy didn't get up. Coach McKenzie and the trainer checked her ankle. Finally, Kathy was helped to the bench. The referee came to the bench. "Coach, you need a player at the free-throw line. She gets two shots."

16 Coach looked at the players on the bench. She'd always stressed the importance of free-throw shooting. Who had paid attention? Kathy, for one. And . . . Abby. She hadn't played much, but she could shoot. "Abby," Coach said. "You're in."

17 Abby's stomach flipped. "Me?" she said. "Now?"

18 Coach leaned closer to her. "I've watched you in practice," she said. "You can do this."

19 Abby jumped up and walked to the foul line. She glanced up at the scoreboard. Two points and a few seconds of defense would win the game. The referee handed Abby the ball. She took a deep breath. Two bounces. She crouched and let the ball fly.

20 *Swish* went the basketball as it entered the hoop. The crowd roared. "One more," Abby thought. She caught the ball. Bounce, bounce. Shoot. The gym exploded with cheers as the ball went in the hoop a second time. Seconds later the buzzer sounded. The Hawks were undefeated, and Abby's time had finally come.

1. What is paragraph 4 mostly about?
   A. Although Abby is on the team, she hardly plays in any games.
   B. Abby is as good a free-throw shooter as Kathy.
   C. Abby dislikes her team.
   D. Abby is a fifth grader on her school's basketball team.

   Objective 1

2. In paragraph 6, the word <u>spared</u> means —
   A. given to
   B. deserving of
   C. helped with
   D. saved from

   Objective 1

3. Read the meanings below for the word <u>trail</u>.

   > **trail** (trāl), *verb*
   > 1. to follow the scent or track of an animal. 2. to follow slowly behind another. 3. to drag along the ground. 4. to be behind an opponent.

   Which meaning best fits the way <u>trailed</u> is used in paragraph 13?
   A. Meaning 1
   B. Meaning 2
   C. Meaning 3
   D. Meaning 4

   Objective 1

4. What is the main problem in the story?
   A. Abby is afraid Coach McKenzie will ask her to leave the team.
   B. Abby is upset that she does not play often enough for the team.
   C. Abby's brother teases her too much.
   D. Abby wants to be as good a basketball player as Kathy.

   Objective 2

5. In the story, why is Abby's mother especially proud of Abby?
   A. Abby helped clear the table after dinner.
   B. Abby had made the school basketball team.
   C. Abby didn't quit the team, even though she hardly got the chance to play.
   D. Abby was a good free-throw shooter.

   Objective 2

6 Read the chart below. It shows the order in which some events happened in the story.

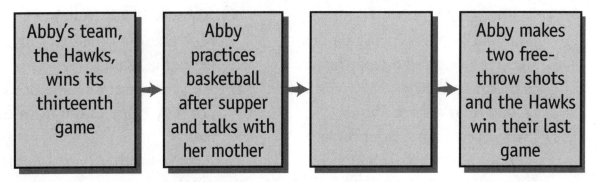

Which of these sentences belongs in the empty box?

A Abby's father takes her brother to a scout meeting.
B Abby waves to her mother on the bleachers.
C Kathy hurts her ankle and is forced to the bench.
D The buzzer sounds, ending the game.

Objective 3

7 Which of the following is the best summary of the story?

A Abby is on the school's winning basketball team. Abby's brother teases her for spending most of her time on the bench. Abby clears the supper table and then practices basketball.

B The Hawks are undefeated. Coach McKenzie congratulates Kathy for her free-throw shots. Abby is good at free-throw shots, too. She wins the final points in the last game of the season.

C Abby's team is undefeated, but Abby rarely plays in games. Although she is sad, her mother tells her to be patient. When Kathy is injured, Abby wins the final game with her free-throw shooting.

D The Hawks are losing their last basketball game by one point. Kathy, one of the team's best players, hurts her ankle while shooting. Abby is called onto the court and wins the game with two free-throw shots.

Objective 1

8 Which of these best describes Abby's feelings in paragraph 5?

A Abby is unhappy to be going home.
B Abby is jealous of Kathy's talent for free-throw shooting.
C Abby is upset that she has not played more this season.
D Abby is angry at Coach McKenzie.

Objective 2

9 Why doesn't Coach McKenzie ask Abby to play in games more often?

A She does not think Abby deserves to be on the team.
B Kathy and Abby are too competitive on the court.
C She is saving Abby for the most difficult plays.
D She thinks the other girls are better players.

Objective 2

10 The author organizes paragraphs 12 through 20 of the story by —

A describing Abby's feelings towards her mother
B narrating events as they occurred in the Hawks' last game
C explaining how school basketball games are played
D comparing Abby with the team's best basketball player

Objective 4

11 Which pair of words best describes Abby's mother?

A Supportive and helpful
B Competitive and funny
C Bossy and interfering
D Jealous and unfriendly

Objective 2

12 The most likely reason the author wrote this story was to —

A explain to readers how basketball is played
B entertain readers with a story about a girl's strength of character
C persuade readers to try out for their school's basketball team
D inform readers about life in an American community

Objective 3

13 Which sentence from the story shows that Abby was upset that she had not played much in games that season?

A *Her throat hurt from cheering.*
B *Abby held back tears as she opened the door.*
C *She held the ball tightly and looked at Mom.*
D *Abby watched as the players ran up and down the court.*

Objective 4

Boys' Life

Vol. 7, Number 5   February 1999

ALONG THE HERD HIGHWAY
by Johnny D. Boggs

1   This wasn't what George Saunders had dreamed about. A year earlier, his two brothers had driven cattle from Texas to Kansas and filled him with stories of adventure. Now George, at seventeen, was on his first real cattle drive.

2   But the thunderstorm was no dream. It was a nightmare. Lightning split the sky, followed by a rumbling noise that chilled even veteran cowboys. Then George heard the panic-filled cry: "Stampede."

3   George spurred his horse and galloped alongside a thousand frightened cattle, praying he wouldn't be trampled as the herd split in several directions. When the longhorns stopped hours later, George was last and alone — except for his horse and 75 cows. As dawn arrived, so did George's boss.

4   The trail boss had taken a chance when he hired the inexperienced cowboy. Would George be fired? They silently drove the longhorns back to the herd. The trail boss said, "Go

Cowboys round up a large herd of cattle

CONTINUED

eat and sleep. You deserve a rest." The boss wasn't mad. George needed the rest. It was still more than 700 miles to Abilene, Kansas.

5 This was life on the Chisholm Trail, the long, dusty route from Texas to the railroads in Kansas. <u>Jesse Chisholm blazed the original trail, but never herded longhorns.</u> Cattlemen used his trail so often that by the 1870s, the 1,000 mile route was known as the Chisholm Trail.

6 Longhorn cattle were plentiful in Texas after the Civil War, and Americans had developed a taste for beef. A cow worth $4 in Texas might fetch $40 in Kansas. As word spread in 1867 that shipping yards in Abilene were ready for cattle, a great American success story began.

7 By the time George Saunders went on his first drive in 1870, the Chisholm Trail was booming. 600,000 longhorns were herded to Kansas that year. By the mid-1880s, an estimated 10 million cattle traveled to Kansas, herded by 35,000 cowboys. Cattle towns like Abilene and Wichita boomed almost overnight.

8 And the legend of the cowboy was born. In the 1870s, teenagers like George dreamed of life on the Chisholm Trail. But they learned quickly that cowboy life was far from glorious.

9 It took about a dozen cowboys and a cook to herd 1,000 to 2,500 cattle on the two to three month journey. The trail boss rode ahead of the herd, and a wrangler drove the extra horses. Usually, the two most experienced cowboys took the lead, or "point" position, followed by two "swing" riders and two on the "flank." The least experienced cowboys got the worst job — riding behind the slowest longhorns to keep the herd moving. There, George and the other "drag" riders breathed little but dust. It was slow — a herd averaged 8 to 10 miles a day — and dull work.

10 With no bridges, cowboys had to drive longhorns into rivers often full of quicksand. George was amazed at the sight before him. With only the animals' heads and horns above water, the herd resembled "a thousand rocking chairs floating on the water."

CONTINUED

11   But the <u>spectacle could turn dangerous in a second</u>. If the longhorns got scared, they might drown. Cowboys had to position themselves in the center of the terrified animals, getting them to swim to shore. In a second, a cowboy could be thrown from his horse into the churning river. George saw the graves on shore, a somber reminder of the dangers along the trail. It was hard work, but they were helping to feed a growing nation.

Jesse Chisholm, for whom the Chisholm Trail was named

THE CHISHOLM TRAIL

1   When Jesse Chisholm blazed the trail that would bear his name, he didn't post signs or road markers. In fact, the trail wasn't well defined except to mark the safest and easiest places to cross rivers and streams.

2   So how did cowboys follow the trail? The first cowboys saw the wagon tracks left by Chisholm when he had hauled goods to Native Americans. Later, pamphlets explained the route and noted landmarks and river crossings. An 1871 government map showed the trail. Details spread by word of mouth so the trail could be followed by travelers, not just cowboys.

3   Today, following the trail is much easier. Four hundred markers, each seven feet high, six inches square and 200 pounds, line the route.

Use "Along the Herd Highway" to answer questions 14–24.

14 What are paragraphs 1 to 4 mainly about?

    A A thunderstorm breaks out over a cattle herd.

    B The Chisholm Trail was the main route cowboys took from Texas to Kansas.

    C George, a new cowboy, tries to help when lightning causes the cattle to stampede.

    D George's boss isn't angry at George even though the cattle have stampeded.

Objective 1

15 In paragraph 3, the word trampled means —

    A discovered by cattle

    B crushed under running feet

    C ignored by the other cowboys

    D dismissed from the cattle drive

Objective 1

16 In paragraph 5, which word helps the reader know what blazed means?

    A dusty

    B original

    C herded

    D used

Objective 1

17 Why is the thunderstorm important to the story in paragraphs 1 to 4?

    A It led the steers to move more quickly towards Kansas.

    B It cost George Saunders his job as a cowboy.

    C It helped the herd to cross the river.

    D It caused a stampede of the longhorns.

Objective 2

18 Read the meaning below for the word spectacle.

> **spectacle** (spek' tə kəl), *noun*
> 1. an incredible sight.
> 2. a lens or eye piece.
> 3. a fireworks show.
> 4. an embarrassing moment in front of others.

Which meaning best fits the way spectacle is used in paragraph 11?

    A Meaning 1

    B Meaning 2

    C Meaning 3

    D Meaning 4

Objective 1

19 Read this outline of information from the story.

> **Along the Herd Highway**
> A. The Chisholm Trail
>   1. Started by Jesse Chisholm
>   2. Thousand miles long
>   3. _____
>   4. Cowboys herded cattle along the trail

Which information belongs on the blank line of the outline?

A George feared his trail boss would be angry.
B It ran from Texas to railroads in Kansas.
C Teenagers dreamed of becoming cowboys.
D Longhorns crossing the river looked amazing.

Objective 3

20 If the longhorns stampeded again, George's trail boss would probably —

A help the men find stray longhorns
B drive the remaining steers to Kansas at a gallop
C fire George from his job as a cowboy
D leave some of the longhorns behind

Objective 4

21 The author organizes paragraphs 5 through 7 of the story by —

A telling some of the history of the Chisholm Trail
B describing George's adventures on his first drive
C narrating a typical day in a cowboy's life
D explaining the problems faced by cowboys on the drive

Objective 4

22 Which sentence from the story shows the reader that cattle herding was not always safe work?

A *This was life on the Chisholm Trail, the long dusty route from Texas to the railroads in Kansas.*
B *But they learned quickly that cowboy life was far from glorious.*
C *The least experienced cowboys got the worst job — riding behind the slowest longhorns to keep the herd moving.*
D *George saw the graves on shore, a somber reminder of the dangers along the trail.*

Objective 4

23 What sight most impressed George Saunders when he reached the river?

- **A** The cowboys in the center of terrified longhorns
- B The hard work of feeding a growing nation
- C A thousand cattle swimming across the river
- D The clouds of dust behind the herd

Objective 2

24 The author tells about the experiences of George Saunders to —

- A make the Chisholm Trail come alive for readers
- B show readers why George Saunders became famous
- C prove to readers that life in the Old West was often very funny
- **D** persuade readers that the Chisholm Trail was often dangerous

Objective 3

Use "The Chisholm Trail" to answer questions 25–26.

25 The selection is mainly about —

- A how cowboys were able to follow the trail
- B what the trail was used for
- C what life was like on the trail
- **D** how the trail is marked today

Objective 1

26 Why did Jesse Chisholm start the trail that bears his name?

- **A** To drive cattle to Kansas
- B To haul goods to Native Americans
- C To help travelers find their way
- D To lead pioneers to new homes

Objective 1

Use "Along the Herd Highway" and "The Chisholm Trail" to answer question 27.

27 How would the cowboys with George Saunders most likely have followed the Chisholm Trail?

- A They followed tracks in the road left by Jesse Chisholm.
- **B** They knew the major landmarks and river crossings.
- **C** They used published government maps.
- D They found help from Native American scouts.

Objective 4

CHILD LIFE
The Children's Own Magazine

April, May 2000 — Vol. 7, Number 5

Elizabeth Blackwell: The First Woman Doctor

1   "Mother, I've finally decided on a career," announced twenty-four year old Elizabeth. "I'm going to study medicine."

2   Mrs. Blackwell accepted this statement calmly. "Are you sure, dear?" she asked. "Remember the bull's eye?"

3   *Oh, I remember all too well, thought Elizabeth!* One day a teacher had brought the eye of a bull into class for a lesson on how the eye works. It came back to her in a flash. She remembered how upset she felt after seeing the eye. Her family had teased her about her squeamishness ever since that day.

Elizabeth Blackwell

4   "I'm sure, Mother," said Elizabeth in a determined way. "I've been thinking about it for some time, and I've made up my mind. I'm going to be doctor."

5   Mrs. Blackwell did not argue with her daughter. She knew Elizabeth had a strong spirit of determination. She was proud of her daughter's decision, even though it seemed quite impossible at the time. She also thought Elizabeth was attracted to medicine just because the mission was impossible. In 1845, a woman doctor was unheard of in America. No medical school would take female students. Besides, Elizabeth had no money. But she did not let either of these things stand in her way. She immediately began working on them.

6   First, she could teach in school to earn money. Soon Elizabeth found a position as a

CONTINUED →

music teacher in a girls' school in Asheville, North Carolina. After a year, she moved to Charleston, South Carolina, where she continued to teach. There she had <u>access</u> to a doctor's library, where she read about medicine. She also kept saving her money.

7 With a tidy sum of money to start her off, Elizabeth moved to Philadelphia and hired a tutor. She persuaded Dr. Warrington, a physician, to let her watch him during the day at his medical practice. With his help, she applied to medical schools in 1847. Some were polite, while others were hostile, but the replies were always the same — No.

8 There was a small college in a little country village in Geneva, New York, at the bottom of the list. Dr. Warrington suggested that she might try there. The head of the college decided to let the medical students themselves decide whether to admit a woman student. He didn't know that his rowdy students were in a playful mood that day. As a joke, they voted to admit Elizabeth to the school.

In 1974, the U.S. Postal Service issued this stamp to honor Elizabeth Blackwell.

9 Blonde and pretty, Elizabeth finally had her chance. She overcame her squeamishness, attended every lecture, earned the respect of other students, and graduated at the top of her class in 1849. Far from being over, her troubles were just starting. While a degree from a two-year medical college might be enough for a man, she knew she would need more training to succeed.

10 She sailed to London, then to France for further study. While working at a Paris hospital, she had an accident that caused her to lose one eye. Now she was forced to give up her plan to study surgery.

CONTINUED

11 So she went to America, where she opened a dispensary (*a medical clinic*) in the slums of New York. Slowly, her patients began to accept her. Then her younger sister Emily finished medical school in Ohio. Emily took further training in Scotland, and came to New York. The two sisters, along with Marie Zachrzewska, a Polish immigrant whom Elizabeth had helped to get a medical education, rented a home on Bleecker Street.

12 On May 12, 1857, they opened the New York <u>Infirmary</u> for Women and Children. Hating the plain, bare look of hospital rooms, they furnished the hospital in a cheerful, homelike fashion. Elizabeth was the director, Emily the surgeon, and Marie the physician. The hospital was a success. Soon other women came to work as interns and residents. Later they even opened their own medical school for women.

13 Elizabeth lived to be more than ninety. She continued to write and lecture until her death. By sheer determination, she overcame all obstacles to make herself into an able physician. In the process, she opened the door for all women doctors who came after her.

---

28 What is the article mostly about?

A The condition of American medical schools 150 years ago

B A woman's struggle to become a doctor

C The struggle of American women to win equal rights with men

D A woman's attempt to overcome her squeamishness

Objective 1

29 What is the most likely reason why the U.S. Postal Service issued a stamp to honor Elizabeth Blackwell in 1947?

A She fought to overcome her squeamishness.

B She traveled more than other women of her time

C She was the first woman in the United States to earn a medical degree.

D She was a gifted and popular music teacher.

Objective 3

30 Which of the following is the best summary of the story?

A Elizabeth is very squeamish as a young girl. She cannot stand seeing a bull's eye in class. When she gets older, she overcomes her squeamishness and becomes the nation's first woman doctor.

B Elizabeth wants to become a doctor. She saves money and is the first woman accepted by an American medical school. She graduates at the top of her class, trains in Europe and later opens up an infirmary in New York.

C After Elizabeth becomes the first woman to graduate from an American school, her sister follows in her footsteps. With Marie Zachrzewska, they open the New York Infirmary for Women and Children. The hospital is a success.

D After earning her medical degree, Elizabeth travels to London and France. In Paris, she works in a hospital but loses her eye in an accident. This forces her to give up her plans to study surgery.

Objective 1

31 In paragraph 3, <u>squeamishness</u> means —

A determination
B feeling ill easily
C being poor
D being cold *Objective 1*

32 In paragraph 13, what does the author mean by Elizabeth's having "opened the door for all women doctors who came after her"?

A Elizabeth often held the door open for other doctors.
B After Elizabeth's success, American women gained the right to vote.
C Elizabeth's success allowed other women to become doctors.
D American women who wanted to study medicine had to attend Elizabeth's New York Infirmary. *Objective 1*

33 The author organizes paragraphs 6 through 11 by —

A explaining how people studied medicine when Elizabeth was in school
B comparing the attitudes of men and women towards doctors
C providing an account of Elizabeth's squeamishness
D narrating a series of important events in Elizabeth's life

Objective 4

34 Read the following definition for the word <u>access</u>.

> **access** (ak' ses), *noun*
> 1. a sudden outburst. 2. an entrance way. 3. the right to enter or make use of something. 4. something that is easy to approach.

Which meaning best fits the way <u>access</u> is used in paragraph 6?

A Meaning 1
B Meaning 2
C Meaning 3
D Meaning 4

Objective 1

35 Look at this web about Elizabeth Blackwell.

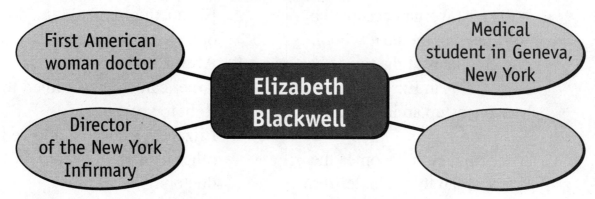

Which of these belongs in the empty oval?

A An average student
B A doctor unable to find patients
C Someone who lost both eyes in an accident
D A student of medicine in Paris, France

Objective 3

36 What was the main reason why Elizabeth decided to teach?

A She wanted to save money to pay for medical school.
B She wanted to help young and needy children.
C She felt it might help her get into medical school.
D She loved to play music.

Objective 3

37 Which would Elizabeth probably **NOT** do as a doctor?

A Give up trying a new treatment because it was difficult
B Work alongside other members of her family
C Help poor children
D Make a hospital look cheerful

Objective 3

38 Look at this timeline showing information from the article.

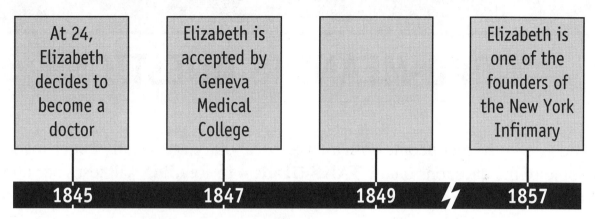

Which of these statements belongs in the empty box?

A Elizabeth teaches music in North Carolina
B Elizabeth watches Dr. Warrington during his medical practice
C Elizabeth becomes America's first woman to earn a medical degree
D Elizabeth helps furnish a hospital in New York City

Objective 3

39 Which statement from the story best illustrates Elizabeth's determination?

A *Mrs. Blackwell did not argue with her daughter.*
B *But she did not let any of those things stand in her way.*
C *Far from being over, her troubles were just starting.*
D *Hating the plain, bare look of hospital rooms, they furnished the hospital in a cheerful, homelike fashion.*

Objective 4

40 What would Elizabeth most likely do if a poor woman with a serious disease wanted to be treated at the New York Infirmary?

A She would refuse to admit the woman.
B She would admit the woman and treat her disease.
C She would send the woman to a different hospital.
D She would first check if the woman could afford to pay for the treatment.

Objective 4

CHAPTER 4

WORD-MEANING QUESTIONS

Did you know that people with a large vocabulary are usually better readers? Some of the questions on the **TAKS Grade 4 in Reading** will test your understanding of the meaning of *a word* or *group of words* used in a reading selection.

DEFINING A WORD

Some *word-meaning questions* will ask you what a word or a group of words means. For example, read the paragraph below. It comes from a famous document in the history of Texas. It is the stirring message that William Travis sent from the Alamo in 1836. Some of the more difficult words in the message are underlined.

> To the people of Texas and all Americans ...
>
> I am <u>besieged</u> by a thousand or more of the Mexicans under Santa Anna. I have <u>sustained</u> a <u>continual</u> <u>bombardment</u> and cannonade for 24 hours and have not lost a man. The enemy has demanded a surrender ..., otherwise the <u>garrison</u> is to be put to the sword, if the fort is taken. I have answered the demand with a cannon shot, and our flag still waves proudly from the walls. I shall never surrender or retreat. Then, I call on you in the name of liberty, of patriotism and everything dear to the American character to come to our aid. ... If this call is <u>neglected</u>, I am determined to ... die like a soldier who never forgets what is due to his own honor and that of his country — victory or death.
>
> *William B. Travis, Commander of the Texas Army*

1   In this passage, the word <u>besieged</u> means —

   A being helped
   B surrounded
   C congratulated
   D followed

How can you answer this question if you do not know the meaning of the word <u>besieged</u>? There are four methods you can use to figure out the meaning of this or any other words you are unsure of.

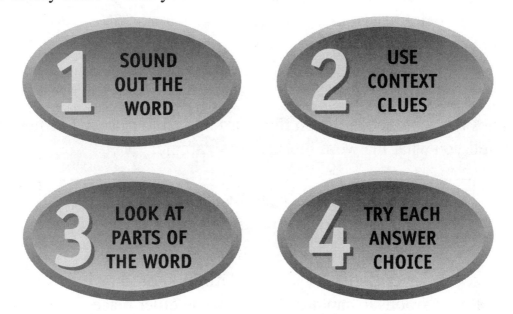

Not every method will always work. However, you can often combine several of these methods to figure out the meaning of an unknown word.

SOUND OUT THE WORD

To sound out a word, say the sounds of the letters that make up the word. By sounding out a word, you may find that it is a word you already know.

Let's try to sound out the word "be-sieged." First break down the word into syllables (*its smaller parts*). Then use the sounds of the letters to say each syllable. Does this sound like any word that you already know? If it does, check the answer choices to see if you can find the correct answer.

USE CONTEXT CLUES

Nearby words and sentences often provide clues to the meaning of a word. These are called **context clues.** On the **TAKS Grade 4 in Reading,** there will always be some context clues to help you answer any *word-meaning question.* In fact, there are several types of context clues you can use to figure out the meaning of an unfamiliar word.

DEFINING CLUES

Sometimes the sentence in which the word appears or nearby sentences will actually tell you what the word means. For example:

> **The Alamo was besieged by surrounding forces who wanted to capture the fort.**

Here, the sentence itself tells you the definition of the word. To *besiege* is to surround with troops to capture a fort or some other place.

CONTRAST CLUES

Sometimes context clues will tell you what a word is *not*. For example:

> **Unlike the frugal Mr. Adams, Ms. Smith spent money every day.**

In this example, the sentence provides an important clue about the meaning of *frugal.* The sentence tells you that Ms. Smith is *not* like Mr. Adams. Ms. Smith *spent money,* while Mr. Adams is *frugal.* From this contrast, you should be able to figure out that the word *frugal* means the opposite of spending *money* — a *frugal* person saves his or her money and spends it very carefully.

COMMON SENSE CLUES

Sometimes you have to use common sense to figure out the meaning of a word. For example:

> **I am besieged by a thousand or more of the Mexicans under Santa Anna.**

Here, the sentence tells you that Travis faces a thousand or more Mexican soldiers who want to take the Alamo. What, then, does **besieged** mean? Your common sense should tell you the meaning of the word.

Let's try a second example from the same passage:

> **The enemy has demanded a surrender ..., otherwise the <u>garrison</u> is to be put to the sword, if the fort is taken.**

What does the word **garrison** mean? The garrison will all be "put to the sword" (*killed*) if Santa Anna's forces take the fort. Who would you expect the Mexican forces to kill? Again, your common sense should tell you that the *garrison* is the group of Texans defending the fort. In this case, you should be able to figure out that a **garrison** is a *group of people guarding or defending a fort*.

You may have to look through the entire paragraph or selection for context clues. Be sure to look at the language used in the selection. It can provide another important clue about the meaning of a word.

★ Is the author telling about something happy or sad?

★ Is the selection funny or serious?

Often the correct answer choice will be the one that best fits with the mood of the reading or the author's viewpoint. For example, the tone of Travis' message is serious and determined as well as stirring and patriotic. In answering *word-meaning questions* about this selection, you should avoid any choices that appear to be overly cheerful, humorous, or cowardly. These would probably not be correct since they are not in keeping with Travis' general message and tone.

PARTS-OF-SPEECH CLUES

Another type of clue is the part of speech of the unfamiliar word. See how this unfamiliar word is used in the sentence. Does it tell about an action (*verb*), name a thing (*noun*), or describe something (*adjective*)? The correct answer should play the same role in the sentence as the unknown word. For example:

> **The fort has survived the enemy's <u>continual</u> bombing.**

Notice how the word **continual** is used in the sentence to describe the enemy's bombing of the fort. The correct answer choice must also be a word or group of words acting as an adjective describing the bombing of the fort.

Sometimes a *word-meaning question* will ask you to identify context clues in the reading selection to answer the question. For example:

2   In Travis' message from the Alamo, which words help the reader know what <u>continual</u> means?

   A   *besieged by a thousand or more*
   B   *for 24 hours*
   C   *have not lost a man*
   D   *demand a surrender*

For this type of question, you need to identify those <u>context clues</u> in the selection that help you figure out the difficult word. In this example, one of the answer choices clearly shows that the fort has been under bombardment that continues for a certain period of time. Which answer choice is it?

LOOK AT PARTS OF THE WORD

Many words are made up of different parts. For example, **homework** brings together the words **home** and **work.**

Some words have special beginnings, called **prefixes**. Knowing certain common *prefixes* can help you figure out the meaning of an unknown word. For example, *re*view, *re*read, *re*turn, and *re*peat all begin with the prefix *re*. Usually *re* in front of a word means "to do again."

Other common prefixes turn a word into its opposite — *un, in,* and *dis* — all mean **not**. You can see this in the following words: *usual* becomes *<u>un</u>usual;* *sincere* changes to *<u>in</u>sincere;* and *similar* turns to *<u>dis</u>similar.* Sometimes a prefix has more than one meaning. The prefix *in* can also mean *inside* — such as *<u>in</u>door.*

Special endings, known as **suffixes,** are also helpful in providing clues about the meaning of an unknown word. For example, *painful* means something that is *full* of pain. *Careful* describes a person who is *full* of care. In those examples, *ful* is the suffix.

Separating the word and its suffix helps you to understand the word. The most common suffixes are *s, ed,* and *ing.* These are simply word endings for plurals of nouns or different tenses of verbs. Other common suffixes change the part of speech of a word — *ly, er, ion, al, ness,* and *ment.*

quick	quick**ly**	govern	govern**ment**
associate	associat**ion**	happy	happi**ness**
continue	continu**al**	teach	teach**er**

Sometimes it helps to cover the front or back of a difficult word to see if you recognize any of its parts. See if you recognize the word without its beginning or ending.

For example, let's look at the word **bombardment** from Travis' message. Do any of this word's parts remind you of other words you know? If you cover the end of the word, you can see the word *bomb.* Is that a word that you know? A *bombardment* is, as you might think, an attack of bombs shot from a cannon or other large gun. *Continual* should remind you of the word *continue* — with a special suffix. Thus, a <u>**continual bombardment**</u> is a constant firing of bombs from cannons or other large guns. Looking at the different parts of a word, when used together with context clues, can often help you to figure out its meaning.

TRY EACH ANSWER CHOICE

The last method for answering a *word-meaning question* is to try putting each answer choice in place of the unfamiliar word. Think about what the author is trying to say in the sentence. Select the word or group of words that seem to make the most sense.

For example, look at the question and answer choices earlier in this chapter on page 41. Read each one in place of *besieged* in the sentence, *"I am besieged by a thousand or more of the Mexicans under Santa Anna."*

> A I am *being helped* by a thousand or more of the Mexicans under Santa Anna.
>
> B I am *surrounded* by a thousand or more of the Mexicans under Santa Anna.
>
> C I am *congratulated* by a thousand or more of the Mexicans under Santa Anna.
>
> D I am *followed* by a thousand or more of the Mexicans under Santa Anna.

★ **Choice A** must be wrong. We know that Mexican soldiers were threatening the fort, not offering to provide help.

★ **Choice C** is wrong. The message does not say that they were congratulating the garrison. In fact, the selection tells us they demanded a surrender or they would put the garrison to the sword.

★ **Choice D** is wrong. The Alamo was not moving anywhere for the Mexican soldiers to follow.

Notice that the message shows that the men in the Alamo were in great distress. Travis ends his message by declaring that the defenders will never surrender and face either victory or death. This only makes sense if they were surrounded by attackers.

SUMMARY: DEFINING A WORD

When you come across an unknown word in a reading, try using these methods to figure out the meaning of the word:

★ <u>Sound out the Word</u>. After you say it, see if you recognize it.

★ <u>Use Context Clues</u>. Look for defining, contrasting, common sense and parts-of-speech context clues.

★ <u>Look at Parts of the Word</u>. See if you recognize the beginning or ending of the word, or the root word without its beginning or ending.

★ <u>Try Each Answer Choice</u>. Read each answer choice in place of the word. Select the answer that makes the most sense.

Now let's practice answering *word-meaning questions*.

THE PENNSYLVANIA DUTCH

1   The "Pennsylvania Dutch" do not come from Holland as their name might suggest. Instead, the Pennsylvania Dutch are the <u>descendants</u> of German immigrants in Pennsylvania who have kept their German language, heritage, and customs. Many of them follow the Amish religion — a form of Protestant Christianity.

2   Today, Lancaster County, Pennsylvania, is the heart of Pennsylvania Dutch country. Small farms cover the hillsides. Thriving vegetable gardens <u>flourish</u> behind the farmhouses. The county <u>resembles</u> almost

CONTINUED

any farming region in America, but on closer inspection, no electric or telephone wires connect houses to lines along the road.

3 Today, the Amish of Lancaster look and live much as they did two hundred years ago. Women's clothes lack zippers and buttons. The Amish consider these too fancy. There is no electrical power for farm work. Horses pull plows across the fields and black buggies into town. Farmhouses sometimes look <u>vacant</u> without curtains or lights in the windows.

1 In paragraph 1, the word <u>descendants</u> means —

   A partners in the same business
   B children and later generations
   C people having the same religion
   D people who have lost their wealth

UNLOCKING THE ANSWER

🗝 **Sound out the word.** [de-scend-ant]
Do you recognize this word?

🗝 **Use context clues.**
- They are descendants of German immigrants.
- They have kept their German language, heritage and customs.

🗝 **Look at parts of the word.** descend-ant
Do any of these parts remind you of any word?
- **Descend** means to *come down*.

🗝 **Try each answer choice.**
Read the choices in place of <u>descendant</u> in the sentence in paragraph 1. Which fits best as the answer?

2 In paragraph 2, which words help us to know what <u>flourish</u> means?

    A *thriving vegetable gardens*
    B *behind farmhouses*
    C *closer inspection*
    D *no electric or phone wires*

UNLOCKING THE ANSWER

This question asks you to select a context clue that helps you to figure out the meaning of the word <u>flourish</u>. For this type of question, you should focus on the surrounding sentences in order to find the correct answer.

- **Use context clues.** *Behind farmhouses*, *closer inspections*, and *no electric or telephone wires* do not provide clues to the definition of ***flourish***. However, a *thriving vegetable garden* — one that is growing well — does provide an important clue to the meaning of the word.

- Based on these clues, what do you think <u>flourish</u> means?

DICTIONARY QUESTIONS

Often, a word will have more than one meaning. Dictionaries list the different parts of speech (*noun, verb, adjective*) that a word might take. Then the dictionary lists the different meanings of the word for each of these parts of speech.

    A special type of *word-meaning question* on the **TAKS Grade 4 in Reading** will ask you to examine a dictionary entry and to select the correct meaning of a word used in the reading selection from that entry. For example, look over the question that appears on the following page. This question is based on a word in the selection on the Pennsylvania Dutch, which you just read.

3 Read the dictionary entry below for the word <u>vacant</u>.

> **vacant** (vā′ kənt), *adj.*
>
> **1.** containing nothing, empty **2.** to be expressionless or blank **3.** a building without anyone living inside **4.** something that has not been claimed

Which meaning best fits the way <u>vacant</u> is used in paragraph 3 (*on the top of page 48*)?

A Meaning 1
B Meaning 2
C Meaning 3
D Meaning 4

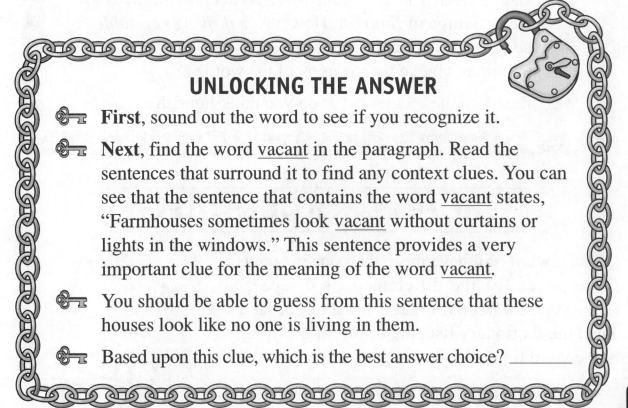

UNLOCKING THE ANSWER

- **First**, sound out the word to see if you recognize it.

- **Next**, find the word <u>vacant</u> in the paragraph. Read the sentences that surround it to find any context clues. You can see that the sentence that contains the word <u>vacant</u> states, "Farmhouses sometimes look <u>vacant</u> without curtains or lights in the windows." This sentence provides a very important clue for the meaning of the word <u>vacant</u>.

- You should be able to guess from this sentence that these houses look like no one is living in them.

- Based upon this clue, which is the best answer choice? _____

GIVE IT A TRY

Now that you have learned how to answer *word-meaning questions,* you should "Give It a Try" by reading the following selection. Then answer the questions.

Mama's Dark World
by Amelia H. Chamberlain

1 It is 6 o'clock in the morning, time to wake up Mama. I open my bedroom door into a wall of darkness. I <u>creep</u> into the living room. The lights are off and the shades are drawn. On the couch lies Mama. Her hair is standing all on ends and her face is a mask of peace. I give her shoulder a shake, telling her that it's 6 o'clock. Instantly, her eyes open and she starts to get up.

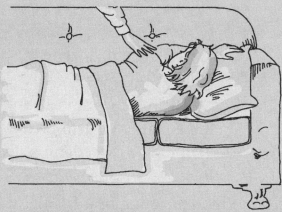

2 I turn to go back to my room, when she asks me to make her a cup of coffee. I <u>swivel</u> around, and a spark of <u>resentment</u> flickers through my eyes. Guilt quickly replaces it. How can I be angry? Every day she gets up and goes to work on four or five, sometimes only two hours of sleep. She even works overtime every chance she gets. I tell her not to push herself, but she says we need the money.

3 All she's asking me for is a cup of coffee. How can I <u>deny</u> her? So I go into the kitchen. I leave the lights off, as if light would be unwelcome in Mama's dark world. I pour a cup of coffee. I take it to her. She's already dressed and sitting up on the couch. I hand her the cup of coffee, and she thanks me.

4 All too quickly, she has to leave. She hands me money for school and kisses me on the cheek. As always, she never forgets to tell me she loves me. Then she walks out the door, off to her job.

CONTINUED

5 I watch from the door in wonder. How does she do it? How does she always remember to leave me money for school? How does she always remember to tell me that she loves me? How does she work all day and do all those errands? How does she raise me and my sisters on her own? She never gives up or says "I can't go today." She never, ever, doesn't get up, no matter how little sleep she's had.

6 I shut and lock the door. I walk silently through Mama's dark world and go back to my bright room. Slowly, I put my head down and think how lucky I am to have Mama.

---

1 Read the meanings below for the word <u>creep</u>.

> **creep** (krēp), *verb*
> **1.** to move about on one's hands and knees **2.** to grow along a surface **3.** to move quietly **4.** to have a tingling sensation

Which meaning best fits the way <u>creep</u> is used in paragraph 1?

A Meaning 1
B Meaning 2
C Meaning 3
D Meaning 4

2 Which word helps the reader to know the meaning of <u>resentment</u> in paragraph 2?

A *spark*
B *eyes*
C *guilt*
D *angry*

3 In paragraph 2, <u>swivel</u> means to —

A rotate
B cheat
C ignore
D look

4 Read the meanings below for the word <u>deny</u>.

> **deny** (dĭ nī′), *verb*
> **1.** to declare that something is not true **2.** to refuse to believe something **3.** to refuse to give **4.** to refuse to recognize

Which meaning best fits the way <u>deny</u> is used in paragraph 3?

A Meaning 1
B Meaning 2
C Meaning 3
D Meaning 4

CHAPTER 5

QUESTIONS ON YOUR BASIC UNDERSTANDING OF A READING

The **TAKS Grade 4 in Reading** will test how well you understand what you read. Two of the ways that the TAKS will test your basic understanding of a reading are the following:

> By asking you what a reading is mostly about

> By asking you to choose the best summary of a reading

The focus of this chapter is to help you answer both of these types of questions.

"MOSTLY ABOUT" QUESTIONS

Some questions on the **Grade 4 TAKS in Reading** will ask you what a reading or part of a reading is "mostly about" or "mainly about." How you answer this type of question will depend on whether the reading selection is a *story* or an *informational reading*.

STORIES

When you see this type of question about a story, it will ask what a paragraph or group of paragraphs is "mostly about." You may recall Question 1 about "Abby Takes Her Shot" in the pretest. This provides an example of a *"mostly about" question* about a story:

1 What is paragraph 4 mostly about?

  A Although Abby is on the team, she hardly plays in any games.
  B Abby is as good a free-throw shooter as Kathy.
  C Abby dislikes her team.
  D Abby is a fifth grader on her school's basketball team.

When you see a *"mostly about" question* about a particular paragraph or group of paragraphs in a story, you should take the following steps:

UNLOCKING THE ANSWER

- **First**, think about what is happening in that paragraph or group of paragraphs. Ask yourself if these paragraphs describe the setting, a character in the story, or tell how a character feels or acts.

- **Next**, see if you can think of a **single sentence** that would best express what is taking place. This sentence should give the main idea of the paragraph or group of paragraphs.

- **Finally**, look at the answer choices. Pick the answer that is closest to your sentence expressing the **main idea** of the paragraph or paragraphs. Answers that give specific details rather than the main idea will **not** be the correct answer. If you are unsure of the correct answer, go back and quickly reread the passage.

Now, let's practice answering a *"mostly about" question* about a story. Read the following selection. Use the steps you have just learned to answer the *"mostly about" question* after the story.

In the following story you should know that a **hare** is a type of rabbit and that a **tortoise** is similar to a turtle except that it lives only on land.

THE HARE AND THE TORTOISE

1   A hare was making fun of a tortoise one day for being so slow. "Do you ever get anywhere?" the hare asked with a mocking laugh. "Yes," replied the tortoise, "and I get there sooner than you think. I'll run you a race and prove it."

2   The hare was very amused at the thought of running a race with the tortoise, and just for fun he agreed to do it. So the fox, who agreed to act as judge, marked the distance for the race and started the runners off.

3   The hare was soon far out of sight. To let the tortoise know how silly it was for him to challenge a speedy hare, the hare decided to lie down beside the course to take a nap until the tortoise could catch up.

4   The tortoise meanwhile kept going slowly but steadily. After a time, the tortoise passed the place where the hare was sleeping. The hare slept on very peacefully. When at last he did wake up, the tortoise was already very near the finishing line. The hare now ran his swiftest, but he could not overtake the tortoise in time.

1   What is paragraph 1 mostly about?

   A   A hare made fun of a tortoise, who then challenged him to a race.
   B   A tortoise was so very slow that other animals were frustrated.
   C   In a mocking tone, a hare made fun of a slow-moving tortoise.
   D   A tortoise and a hare had a race to see who was the faster runner.

2   Paragraph 4 is mostly about —

   A   why the hare decided to take a nap
   B   how the tortoise won the race
   C   why the hare awoke from his nap
   D   how the hare ran swiftly at the end of the race

INFORMATIONAL READINGS

As you learned in Chapter 2, an informational reading usually has a *main idea* and *supporting details.* A *"mostly about" question* about an informational reading may ask you for the main idea of the selection as a whole or the main idea of several paragraphs. Question 28 about the article "Elizabeth Blackwell" in the pretest was an example of this type of question:

> **28** What is the article mostly about?
>
> **A** The condition of American medical schools 150 years ago
> **B** A woman's struggle to become a doctor
> **C** The struggle of American women to win equal rights with men
> **D** A woman's attempt to overcome her squeamishness

When you see a *"mostly about" question* that asks about an informational reading as a whole, use the steps outlined below.

UNLOCKING THE ANSWER

- **First**, think about the topic or subject matter of the reading. Often the title will tell you its topic.

- **Next**, think about the chief message of the reading about that topic. Try to think of a *sentence* that expresses the main idea of what you read. Sometimes the reading itself will state the main idea in a topic sentence at the beginning or end of the selection.

- **Finally**, look at the answer choices. Pick the answer closest to your sentence expressing the main idea. Remember, answers that give specific details rather than the main idea are usually **not** correct.

If the question asks for the main idea of a **paragraph** or **group of paragraphs,** use the same steps as you would for a *"mostly about"* question for a story. Let's practice answering a *"mostly about" question* for an informational reading.

Vol. 28, Number 12   **August, 2001**

WHEN MONEY GREW ON TREES
by Amy Butler Greenfield

1   Several thousand years ago, forest dwellers in Central America discovered an amazing tree in the rain forest. Small white flowers sprang from its branches and its trunk. The flowers ripened into red-and-yellow fruit. This fruit contained seeds, or beans, that humans could eat. The small brown beans were bitter, but had a flavor the forest dwellers liked.

2   By 500 B.C., people in Mexico and Central America were growing these cacao trees. Over time cacao beans became quite valuable — so valuable that the great Aztec rulers collected them as a tax. By the later 1400s, people were treating these beans like coins; they used them to buy food and clothing.

3   Cacao beans had other good points. They were cheap enough to be used for small purchases and usually lasted for several years. More importantly, unlike coins, cacao beans could be eaten.

4   People with extra cacao beans drank *cacahuatl* (ka-ka-hwa-tel), a mixture of ground-up cacao beans, cold water, corn, and chili peppers. Some people liked to add vanilla and flowers to the mixture. Often they dyed the drink red. But no matter what color it was, *cacahuatl* was very spicy — and bitter! It didn't taste like the chocolate that we know today.

CONTINUED

5   Europeans first saw cacao beans in 1502, when Christopher Columbus and his son Ferdinand stumbled across them. Neither of them understood how valuable the beans were. In 1519, however, when Cortés invaded Mexico, he discovered warehouses filled with cacao beans in the royal stronghold. Soon the Spaniards realized that cacao beans were like money in the Americas — money that grew on trees!

6   Dreaming of riches, the Spaniards forced the native people to grow more and more cacao beans. Cacao beans poured into the conquerors' storehouses, even as the native people — and their land — suffered greatly.

7   To the Spaniards, cacao beans were money, not food. They refused to drink *cacahuatl*. They thought it looked like dirty water. When it was dyed red, some of the Spaniards felt it looked like blood.

8   In time, however, the Spaniards created their own version of the drink. They called it chocolate. Like the Aztec *cacahuatl*, Spanish chocolate was made with cacao beans, chili peppers, vanilla, and water. But unlike *cacahuatl*, chocolate did not have corn. Instead, it had sugar.

9   By the 1580s, the new beverage was very popular. People in the Spanish colonies sent cacao beans to friends back in Spain so they could make chocolate, too. Their friends enjoyed the unusual beverage, but they made a few changes to it. Although some people in Spain continued to make chocolate with cold water, others preferred the drink hot. Many Spaniards added extra sugar to the recipe. Others added cinnamon and cloves.

10   Word of the drink spread to the rest of Europe. Over the next decades, Europeans added almonds, egg yolks, lemon peel, nutmeg, and melon seeds to their chocolate. They also added an ingredient very familiar to us today: milk. To these people, cacao beans were food, not money. They never tried to use the beans as coins, and eventually the people of Spanish America stopped using them as currency, too.

3 What is this article mostly about?

    A The use of cacao beans changed from a form of money to an ingredient in a sweet drink.
    B The Aztecs used cacao beans as a form of money.
    C The Aztecs used cacao beans to make *cacahuatl,* a spicy drink that was dyed red.
    D The Spanish added sugar to crushed cacao beans.

Before you select an answer to this question, let's see if we can point you in the right direction. Answer the questions below. They will help lead you to the correct answer choice.

POINTING THE WAY

➡ What is the **topic** of the reading? _____
_____

➡ What is the author's **main idea** about this topic? _____
_____

➡ Which answer choice is most like your main idea above? _____

SUMMARY QUESTIONS

Some questions on the **TAKS 4 in Reading** will ask you to choose the best **summary** of the reading. To **summarize** means to retell what is in the reading in a shorter form. A **summary** gives the *main ideas* and *most important details,* while leaving out less important information. *Summary questions* test your ability to separate important information from less important information.

SUMMARIZING A STORY

On the next page is an example of a *summary question* based on the story "Abby Takes Her Shot," which appeared on the pretest.

7 Which of the following is the best summary of the story?

   A Abby is on the school's winning basketball team. Abby's brother teases her for spending most of her time on the bench. Abby clears the supper table and then practices basketball.
   B The Hawks are undefeated. Coach McKenzie congratulates Kathy for her free-throw shots. Abby is good at free-throw shots, too. She wins the final points in the last game of the season.
   C Abby's team is undefeated, but Abby rarely plays in games. Although she is sad, her mother tells her to be patient. When Kathy is injured, Abby wins the final game with her free-throw shooting.
   D The Hawks are losing their last basketball game by one point. Kathy, one of the team's best players, hurts her ankle while shooting. Abby is called onto the court and wins the game with two free-throw shots.

As you learned in Chapter 2, a story usually tells how its characters try to overcome some problem. A good summary of a story therefore identifies:

- **the central problem faced by the characters**
- **how the characters resolve the central problem**

In this case, the central problem is that Abby, although a member of the winning Hawks, is hardly ever called on to play in any games. Her unhappiness is further stirred by her brother, who continually teases her about her lack of playing time on the court. As the story develops, we learn how Abby handles this problem. Her mother tells Abby to be patient because her time to shine will come. Eventually, it does. Only one of the answer choices above correctly identifies this central problem and tells how it is finally resolved.

When you are faced with a *summary question* about a story, you should take the steps outlined on the next page to find the correct answer choice.

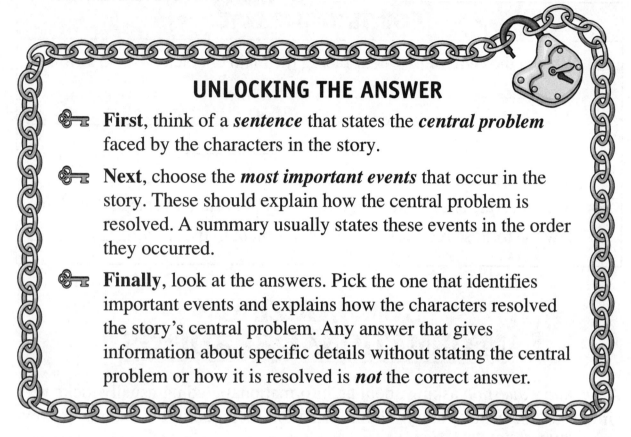

UNLOCKING THE ANSWER

- **First**, think of a *sentence* that states the *central problem* faced by the characters in the story.

- **Next**, choose the *most important events* that occur in the story. These should explain how the central problem is resolved. A summary usually states these events in the order they occurred.

- **Finally**, look at the answers. Pick the one that identifies important events and explains how the characters resolved the story's central problem. Any answer that gives information about specific details without stating the central problem or how it is resolved is *not* the correct answer.

Let's practice answering a *summarizing question* about a story. Reread the story, "The Hare and the Tortoise," on page 55. Then answer the question below.

4 Which of the following is the best summary of the story?

A A hare makes fun of a tortoise for being slow. The tortoise challenges the hare to a race. Although the hare is much faster, the tortoise wins the race.

B A tortoise and a hare have a race. The fox acts as judge of the race. The hare decides to take a nap in the middle of the race. The tortoise passes the hare but does not wake him up.

C A tortoise challenges a hare who was made fun of him to a race. The hare runs far ahead but decides to take a nap. Although slower, the tortoise keeps moving along. He passes the sleeping hare and wins the race.

D A speedy hare is amused at the thought of having a race with a much slower tortoise. The fox agrees to act as judge. The animals are all surprised when the tortoise finally wins the race.

Use the hints on the following page to help you find the correct answer.

POINTING THE WAY

➡ What is the **central problem** facing the main character — the tortoise?
_____

➡ How is the problem in the story **resolved?** _____
_____
_____

➡ Now, pick the answer that best identifies important events and explains how the tortoise resolves the central problem in the story. _____

SUMMARIZING INFORMATIONAL READINGS

A *summary question* asking about an informational reading usually looks very similar to one about a story. The information included in the summary, however, will be different. It should state the reading's *main idea* and include any *important details* needed to explain or support the main idea. Less important details should be left out.

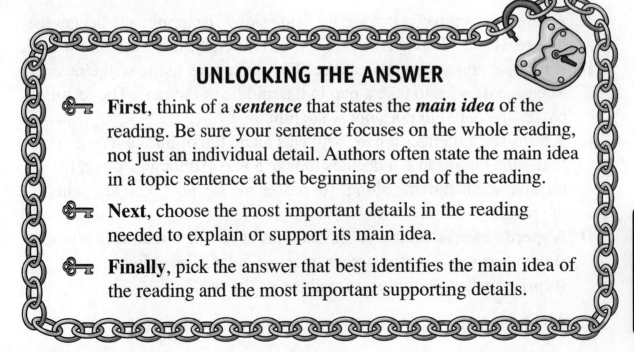

UNLOCKING THE ANSWER

🔑 **First**, think of a *sentence* that states the *main idea* of the reading. Be sure your sentence focuses on the whole reading, not just an individual detail. Authors often state the main idea in a topic sentence at the beginning or end of the reading.

🔑 **Next**, choose the most important details in the reading needed to explain or support its main idea.

🔑 **Finally**, pick the answer that best identifies the main idea of the reading and the most important supporting details.

CHAPTER 5: QUESTIONS ON YOUR BASIC UNDERSTANDING OF A READING 63

Now let's practice answering a *summary question* about an informational reading. Reread the article. "When Money Grew on Trees," on pages 57–58. Then answer the following question.

5 Which is the best summary of the article?

A The Aztecs made a bitter, spicy drink known as *cacahuatl*. They mixed ground-up cacao beans, cold water, corn, and chili peppers. Some people added vanilla and flowers, and dyed the drink red. Spaniards thought it looked like blood.

B The uses of cacao beans have changed over time. Aztecs used cacao beans as money but also to make *cacahuatl,* a spicy, bitter drink. Spaniards used the beans to make the sweet drink we call chocolate.

C Forest dwellers ate bitter cacao beans because they liked the taste. Later Native Americans crushed the beans and mixed them with cold water, corn, and chili peppers to make a spicy drink. They also used cacao beans as a form of money.

D Money has taken many different forms. The Aztecs used cacao beans as a form of money. The Spanish conquerors later kept these cacao beans in storehouses.

Follow the suggestions below to find the correct answer.

POINTING THE WAY

➡ Write a *sentence* that expresses the *main idea* of the reading. _____

➡ List the most *important details* in the reading needed to explain or support this main idea. _____

➡ Now pick the answer that best identifies the *main idea* of the reading and tells the most important details. _____

GIVE IT A TRY

Let's put what you have just learned to the test. Read the following selection and answer the questions after it. These questions are based on both this chapter and the previous chapter on *word-meaning questions*.

The Lion's Whisker

1   Once there lived a husband and wife in a small village in Ethiopia, Africa. The husband was not happy with their marriage. He often came home late from his work in the fields. Sometimes he failed to come home at all to his wife.

2   His wife loved him very much, but she was also unhappy in their relationship. She finally decided to talk to the oldest and wisest man in the village. The old man had married them ten years earlier, and now she asked him to end the marriage.

3   The village elder listened patiently to her bitter words and responded with kindness. "Separation is not always the best choice, my dear. I know of a far better way. I will prepare a secret potion that will change your husband into an obedient and loving man. He will come home on time and always try to please you."

4   "Prepare this wonderful medicine at once, old man!" cried the woman. For truly, she wanted to stay married.

5   "Ah, that is not easy to do," replied the wise man. "I lack one vital ingredient to make the potion. I need a single whisker taken from a living lion. If you bring me such a whisker, I will prepare my secret <u>potion</u> for you to drink."

CONTINUED

6 "I will get it for you," she said with <u>determination</u>.

7 The following morning, the woman carried a large chunk of raw meat down to the river where lions often came to drink. Hiding behind a clump of bushes, she patiently waited quietly until a lion appeared.

8 The woman was quite frightened of the lion and wanted to run away, but she found the courage to toss the meat to the hungry beast. The lion quickly <u>devoured</u> the meat in three gulps and walked slowly back into the trees. The woman fed the lion the next morning and every morning that week. During the second week, she crept out of hiding and let the lion see who was bringing his breakfast.

9 By the third week, she moved closer and closer to the feeding lion. When four weeks had passed, she was able to sit down quietly next to him while he ate. The lion grew comfortable in her presence. Thus, it became possible for her to reach over gently one day and pluck a single whisker from the lion's chin.

10 She ran to the wise man with her prize and pleaded with him to make the secret potion at once. He was surprised to see the lion's whisker, and demanded to know how the woman had <u>acquired</u> it.

11 After hearing her story, the old man said, "You do not need magic to change the ways of your husband. You are brave enough to pull a single whisker from a living lion. It was a dangerous task that required cleverness, courage, and patience. If you can accomplish this, why not use that same courage, patience, and skill to improve your marriage?"

CONTINUED

12 "Don't get angry with your husband, but show him each day that you love him. Gently point out that you, too, want to be respected and loved. Share his problems and make him feel wanted. Give him time to change and see what will happen."

13 The woman went home that day and put the old man's advice to work. Slowly, the relationship between her and her husband began to improve. Within a year, their marriage grew into one of happiness that could last for a lifetime.

---

1 What are paragraphs 1 and 2 of the story mostly about?

~~A~~ A man and woman were happily married in Ethiopia.
(B) A woman went to the village elder to end her unhappy marriage.
~~C~~ A powerful village elder controlled everything that took place in his village.
~~D~~ A woman was patient enough to pluck a whisker from a lion.

2 In paragraph 10, <u>acquired</u> means —

~~A~~ gained — ganado
(B) brought — traido
~~C~~ stole — robado
~~D~~ sold — vendido

3 Look at the following dictionary meaning for the word <u>determination</u>.

> **determination**
> (dē' ter mĭ nā shun), *noun*
> 1. the ending of something
> 2. a decision solving a dispute 3. a judgement
> 4. strength of purpose

Which meaning best fits the way <u>determination</u> is used in paragraph 6?

~~A~~ Meaning 1
B Meaning 2
~~C~~ Meaning 3
(D) Meaning 4

4 In paragraph 8, what does the word <u>devoured</u> mean?

- A. Grabbed
- B. Buried
- C. Ate
- D. Spit at

5 In paragraph 5, <u>potion</u> means —

- A. liquid mixture
- B. cold soda
- C. a part of something
- D. refreshing beverage

6 What are paragraphs 12 and 13 of the story mostly about?

- A. A woman tries to save her marriage.
- B. A woman faces problems in her unhappy marriage.
- C. The village elder tells a woman how to save her marriage.
- D. A woman is rewarded for capturing a lion's whisker.

7 Read the first sentence in the summary below. Then answer the question that follows.

> **Summary**
> A woman is unhappy with her marriage.

Which set of sentences best finishes the summary of this story?

- A. She goes to the village elder, who offers to make a secret potion to make her husband love her. When she brings him the missing ingredient, the wise man is unable to make the potion.
- B. She is told she must get the whisker of a living lion to make her husband love her. For several weeks she feeds a lion raw meat. When the lion gets used to her, she plucks the whisker while the lion is eating.
- C. She wants to end it but changes her mind when she learns a secret potion can make her husband love her. To make the secret potion, she must get the whisker of a living lion.
- D. She goes to the village wise man to end it. He promises to mix a secret potion to make her husband love her if she can bring him a lion's whisker. When she shows patience and wisdom in getting the whisker, he tells her to use the same skills with her husband.

CHAPTER 6

QUESTIONS ON THE ELEMENTS OF A STORY

Some questions on the reading test will ask you about the **setting, characters** or **plot** of a story. In this chapter, you will learn how to answer these kinds of questions. Let's begin by reading a story similar to those on the actual test. The rest of the chapter will use this story as a basis for sample questions.

Highlights for Children
A MAGAZINE FOR CHILDREN

February, 1999 Vol. 9, Number 6

THE RECITAL
by Kathleen Benner Duble

1 "Hannah?" Mama said. "Are you all right?"

2 Hannah nodded yes. But it wasn't true. Since this morning her stomach had been doing flips like that day on the water slide when it kept going faster and faster and wouldn't slow down. When she had reached the bottom, she threw up in front of millions of people. Thinking of this made Hannah feel even sicker.

3 "You're not nervous, are you?" Mama said. Hannah shook her head no.

CONTINUED →

4 "Why would she be scared?" Mary piped up. "She only has to play 'Twinkle, Twinkle, Little Star.' It's so easy I never practice it anymore. Besides, I'll be playing it with her. I'm the one who should be scared."

5 At the mention of "Twinkle," Hannah felt her stomach turn again. She thought of the piano waiting at Mrs. Johnson's studio, and her mouth suddenly felt dry and sticky. Mary picked up her violin and began to play. It sounded beautiful to Hannah. It was something that would be too hard for her to play.

6 "I should be nervous," Mary said, "I have to play three pieces tonight. But I'm not scared."

7 Hannah knew Mary was not scared. Mary was never scared. Hannah wished she were more like Mary. Hannah stared at her own white blouse, dark skirt, white tights, and black shoes. She felt like a zebra.

8 Papa came into the room and scooped up Mary. "So, it's the big night, is it? I can't wait to hear my little musicians play." He grinned at Hannah. Hannah forced herself to smile back.

9 Papa hugged her against him, still holding Mary. "To the car," he said, "and on to Mrs. Johnson's studio."

10 Backstage, Hannah's hands were cold and damp. She felt on edge. All around, students were tuning their instruments. Hannah peeked through the closed curtains at the stage. The stage looked huge. The piano looked as if it could open its lid and eat her.

11 "Places, everyone!" called Mrs. Johnson. Mary danced into line behind Hannah and the other younger children.

12 "Aren't you supposed to be back here with us, Mary?" an older girl whispered.

CONTINUED

13 "I have to play with my sister first," Mary whispered. "Then I'll be back." Mary put her hand in Hannah's and squeezed it tight. "It'll be all right," she said softly. Weakly, Hannah squeezed back.

14 The curtain opened. One child played, then another. Soon, Hannah heard Mrs. Johnson announce her name and Mary's name. Slowly she walked on to the stage with Mary behind her. Hannah's legs felt weak. The lights were bright.

15 Quickly, Hannah walked to the piano. Mary stood by her, and they bowed. There was clapping. Again, Hannah felt an awful taste in her mouth. When the clapping stopped, Hannah slid onto the piano bench. Mary put her violin to her chin and smiled at Hannah.

16 Mary and Hannah began to play. She thought about playing and nothing else. Suddenly, Hannah heard something odd. Mary was not playing "Twinkle." Hannah didn't know what Mary was playing. Hannah couldn't believe Mary was making a mess out of "Twinkle."

17 Hannah glanced at Mary. Her face was white, and her hands were trembling on the violin. Then Hannah realized that Mary had forgotten the notes, and was now scared.

18 "I should have practiced," Mary thought, almost crying. Hannah began whispering the notes to Mary — *A, A, E, E, F-sharp* …. Slowly, Mary hit the notes in time with Hannah's playing. When they finished, they finished together.

19 The clapping was loud in Hannah's ears. When they bowed, Hannah took Mary's hand. Mary's hand was damp and cold, but Hannah's hand was dry and warm. Backstage, Mary didn't say a word, but ran off to be with her friends.

20 "Were you nervous?" someone asked Mary. "Who, me?" said Mary, "I'm never scared."

21 Just then, Mary turned and caught Hannah's eye. Mary smiled, and Hannah smiled. Hannah would never tell. Mary was her sister. Deep inside Hannah felt comforted knowing Mary, too, could be scared.

QUESTIONS ABOUT THE STORY SETTING

The **setting** is *where* and *when* the story takes place. Questions on the setting of a story may ask you to:

- **identify the time or place of the story**
- **tell why the time or place of the story is important**

For an example of the first type of question, answer the following:

1 Where are the characters at the beginning of the story?

  A At a piano recital
  B In Hannah and Mary's house
  C In Mrs. Johnson's studio
  D In a car on the way to the recital

For questions that ask you to ***identify*** the ***time*** or ***place*** of a story, use the following approach:

UNLOCKING THE ANSWER

- **First**, look for clues in the story about *when* and *where* it takes place. These clues are often found at the beginning of the story. Remember that a story may be set in more than one time and place. Be aware that the setting of the story can often change as the story unfolds.

- **Next**, if the setting is not described directly, it may be possible to guess at the setting from the descriptions, actions, or speech of the characters.

- **Finally**, if you do not find information about the setting of the story at the beginning, look through the story to find more details.

HOW TO LOOK FOR DETAILS IN A READING SELECTION

To answer questions about *setting, character,* or *plot,* you will sometimes need to look through a selection quickly to find specific information:

★ Look over each paragraph while hunting for **key words.** Keep your eyes looking for key words without getting too caught up in what you read. Stop each time you spot a name or description you are looking for. For example, if you are trying to find the story setting, stop every time you see the name or description of a place or a time.

★ Each time you stop, read that section carefully for details. See if it provides the information you need to answer the question.

★ If you have not found the answer, then continue looking for the next place where the setting might be discussed.

This method of looking for specific information in a reading selection is known as **scanning.** Think of scanning as a treasure hunt. You are searching through the reading to find a piece of buried treasure.

Some questions may ask why the setting of a story is important:

2   Why is it important that the story ends at a recital?

   A   It permits the parents to hear their daughter play in public.
   B   It helps Hannah learn that Mary can get scared, too.
   C   It reminds Hannah of the water slide.
   D   It shows the importance of Mrs. Johnson to the story.

CHAPTER 6: QUESTIONS ON THE ELEMENTS OF A STORY

UNLOCKING THE ANSWER

To answer a question about why the setting of a story is important:

- **First**, decide *where* and *when* the story takes place.
- **Next**, think about how the time and place of the story help make events in the story happen. Often, the central problem is shaped by the story's time and place. Could the events in the story have occurred in another place or time?
- **Finally**, look over the answer choices. See which one best explains how the time or place of the story helped make story events happen.

QUESTIONS ABOUT THE CHARACTERS

On the reading test, you may find questions about the characters in a story:

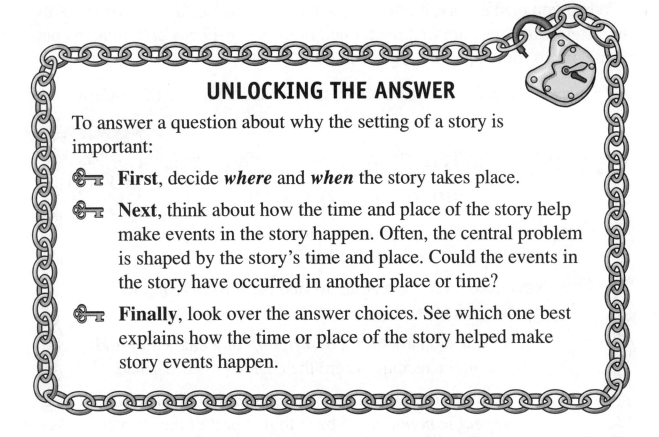

- Who are the characters, and what are they like?
- What are the relationships among the characters with one another?
- Why do the characters feel and act as they do?
- How are the characters changed by what happens in the story?

When you read a story, it often helps to circle or underline the names of the characters when they are first mentioned in the story. Focus on the main characters. Try to form a picture in your mind of what each main character is like.

To answer a specific question about story characters, take these steps:

UNLOCKING THE ANSWER

- **First**, study the question. Be sure that you fully understand what the question is asking for.

- **Next**, look over the reading to find the information the question asks for.
  - If the question asks for a *description* of a character, find places in the reading where the character is described.
  - If the question asks how a character *thinks*, *feels*, or *acts* at a *specific moment*, go back to that part of the story to find the answer.
  - If the question asks how a character is *changed* by an event in the story, find that event in the story. Reread that section of the story to see how the character is changed.

- Sometimes the information you need may **not** be stated directly in the reading. For example:
  - You may have to decide how a character *thinks* or *feels* based on how he or she *acts* in the story.
  - You may have to decide how a character is *changed* by an event based on how that character *acts afterwards*.

- **Finally**, look over the answer choices and pick the one that you think best answers the question.

Now, let's practice answering questions about characters. The following questions are based on "The Recital," which you just read.

3   Look at these pictures of a girl's face.

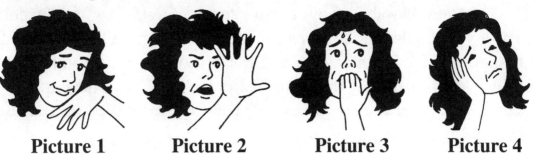

Which picture best shows how Hannah is feeling in paragraph 5?

A   Picture 1   C   Picture 3
B   Picture 2   D   Picture 4

> To answer the question correctly, you need to reread paragraph 5 to remind yourself how Hannah feels. Paragraph 5 shows that Hannah is nervous. Her stomach is turning, and her mouth is dry and sticky. Hannah is clearly worried as she thinks about the piano recital later that day. The best answer is therefore picture 3 — someone feeling nervous.

4   Which word best describes how Hannah's sister, Mary, felt before going to the piano recital?

A   tired   C   confident
B   worried   D   bored

> To answer the question correctly, review the reading to find paragraphs that describe Mary's actions and feelings before going to the recital. Paragraph 4 contains a clue to Mary's feelings. Here she makes light of the fact that she has to play at the recital. What do you think makes the best answer choice?

5   What does Hannah do to help her sister Mary at the recital?

A   She holds her violin.
B   She squeezes Mary's hand.
C   She helps Mary to practice.
D   She whispers musical notes to her.

> This question asks about how a character acts. Again, to find the correct answer you should reread that part of the selection that tells about what the question asks for. Paragraphs 17 and 18 tell about the recital and how Hannah helps her sister Mary during the performance. What is the best answer?

6 How is Hannah changed by what happened at the recital?

  A She wishes to give up playing the piano.
  B She refuses to ever perform with her sister again.
  C She realizes others can be nervous too.
  D She wants to learn how to play the violin.

> This question looks at how a character is changed by an event in the story. Here, you need to review events during and after the recital. Paragraphs 20 and 21 have information about how Hannah has been changed. What is the best answer choice?

7 How does Mary view her playing with Hannah at the recital?

  A She believes she played well.
  B She realizes that she should have practiced.
  C She thinks the recital began too early.
  D She sees the song as more difficult than she thought.

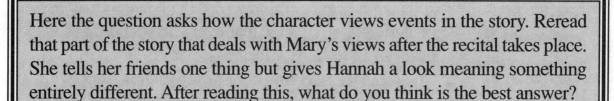

> Here the question asks how the character views events in the story. Reread that part of the story that deals with Mary's views after the recital takes place. She tells her friends one thing but gives Hannah a look meaning something entirely different. After reading this, what do you think is the best answer?

QUESTIONS ABOUT THE PLOT

The **plot** is the series of events that take place in a story. Usually, the main characters face some problem they must solve. Questions about plot on the **Grade 4 TAKS in Reading** will often focus on the central or main problem of the story. They may ask you:

CHAPTER 6: QUESTIONS ON THE ELEMENTS OF A STORY   77

- to identify the central problem faced by the story characters
- to tell how these events help the characters solve the central problem
- to recognize important events in the story

IDENTIFYING THE CENTRAL PROBLEM

One type of question about plot will ask you to identify the *central problem* of the story.

UNLOCKING THE ANSWER

To answer this kind of question, use the following steps:

- **First**, read through the story to determine the major problem the characters face. Often it is presented early in the reading. Try to state this problem in a sentence.

- **Next**, look carefully at the main events in the story. See if most of these events influence the ability of the characters to solve the central problem. If they do not, you may not have stated the central problem correctly. For example, many events and details in "The Recital" have to do with Hannah's nervousness.

- **Finally**, look at the answer choices. Pick the one that best describes the central problem.

Apply these steps to answer the following question about "The Recital."

8 What is the main problem in the story?

   A Mary does not like to practice the violin.
   B Hannah is nervous about performing at a recital.
   C Hannah is jealous of her sister Mary.
   D Mary refuses to perform with her younger sister.

SEQUENCE QUESTIONS

Some questions about plot may ask you about the sequence, or order, of events:

- What happened *before* or *after* an event in the story?
- Which event happened *first* or *last*?
- Which is the correct order of events in the story?

To answer a question about the sequence of events, take the following steps:

UNLOCKING THE ANSWER

- **First**, find the events listed in the question.
- **Next**, pay close attention to the order of those events. Remember, most writers present events in the order in which they are supposed to have taken place. The author always tells you if an event is out of sequence — for example, if a character remembers something from the past.
  - You might number the events in the reading or make a list of the order in which they happened.
  - You could make a diagram, such as a timeline, showing the order of events in the story.
- **Finally**, look over the answer choices. Pick the answer that states the correct order of events.

Let's try answering a *sequence question* about "The Recital."

9   Which event in the story happened first?

   A   Mary played a beautiful piece of violin music.
   B   Hannah's stomach was doing flips.
   C   The family got in the car to go to the recital.
   D   Mrs. Johnson told the performers to take their places.

CHAPTER 6: QUESTIONS ON THE ELEMENTS OF A STORY   79

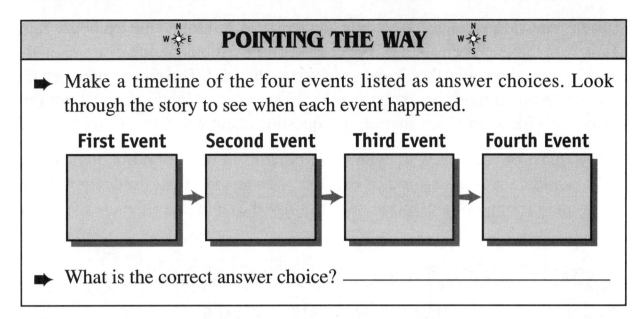

CAUSE-AND-EFFECT QUESTIONS

Some questions about plot on the **Grade 4 TAKS in Reading** may ask *why* an event in the story takes place or why the event is important. These kinds of questions require you to understand **cause and effect.**

★ The **cause** of something is what made it happen. For example, if you turn on a light switch, you cause the light to go on. Questions asking for a cause often begin with the word *why.*

★ The **effect** of something is what happens as a result. The effect of your turning on the light switch is that the light goes on.

Often, key words in the reading will help you answer the question. These key words include: ***why, because, as a result,*** and ***in order to.*** Sometimes you will not find these key words in the reading, but it will still be clear that one event caused another.

If the question asks *why* something happened, look through the reading. Quite often something happens in a story because of the actions of one or more characters. Think about why the characters acted as they did. The *reason why* a character did something often explains *why* it happened. Always think about the motives of characters when answering a question about why an event took place.

If a question asks why an event is *important* to the story, the question is really asking about the *effects* of the event. To answer this, think about how the event or its effects help the characters solve the central problem in the story.

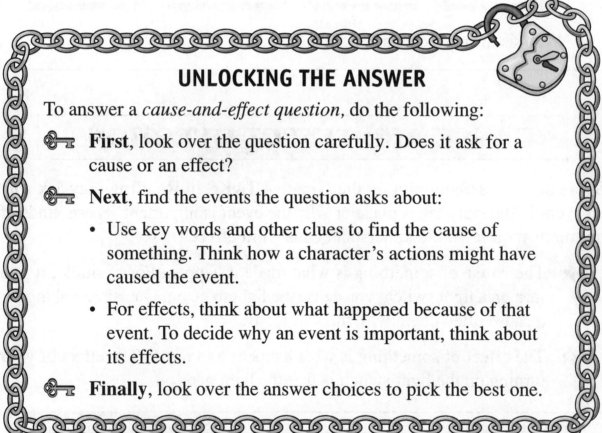

UNLOCKING THE ANSWER

To answer a *cause-and-effect question*, do the following:

- **First**, look over the question carefully. Does it ask for a cause or an effect?

- **Next**, find the events the question asks about:
  - Use key words and other clues to find the cause of something. Think how a character's actions might have caused the event.
  - For effects, think about what happened because of that event. To decide why an event is important, think about its effects.

- **Finally**, look over the answer choices to pick the best one.

Let's practice answering a *cause-and-effect question*. Answer the following question about "The Recital":

10 Why did Mary forget the notes to "Twinkle, Twinkle Little Star"?

    A The song was too difficult for her.
    B She was too busy helping Hannah to think about it.
    C She was too nervous to think about the song.
    D She did not practice the song because it seemed easy.

CHAPTER 6: QUESTIONS ON THE ELEMENTS OF A STORY   81

> This question asks why an event happened. To answer this question correctly, you need to review the story to see which events in the plot led Mary to forget the notes. Which event in the story best explains why Mary did not know the notes at the recital?

GIVE IT A TRY

The following excerpt comes from the first chapter of the book *Josefina Learns a Lesson* by Valerie Tripp. Read the selection and answer the questions that follow.

"LIGHT AND SHADOW"

1   "Mariá Josefina Montoya!" said Tía [*aunt*] Dolores happily. "How beautiful you look!" Josefina blushed and smiled at her aunt. "Gracias," [*thank you*] she said. She smoothed the long skirt of her new dress with both hands. The cotton material felt soft and light. Josefina rose up on her toes and spun, just for the sheer pleasure of it. She was very proud of her dress, which she had just finished hemming. She had never had a dress made in this elegant, new, high-waisted style before.

2   Tía Dolores had given Josefina and each of her sisters some material. Josefina's material was a pretty yellow, with narrow stripes and tiny berries on

it. She had cut her material carefully, the way Mamá had taught her. Then stitch by tiny stitch, she had sewn her dress together all by herself. Now, as she spun around, the hearth fire cast a pattern of light and shadow swooping across the dress like a flock of fluttering birds.

[CONTINUED]

3   Josefina stopped spinning and sighed with peaceful contentment. It was a rainy evening in October. Josefina and her three older sisters, Ana, Francisca, and Clara, were sewing in front of the fire in the family *sala* [*large room*]. Tía Dolores was helping them. They were glad of the fire's warmth and cheerful brightness. A steady rain was falling outside, but inside it was cozy. The thick, whitewashed *adobe* [*building of earth mixed with straw and water*] walls kept out the cold and took on a rosy glow from the firelight.

4   Tía Dolores sat next to Clara. "Don't use such a long thread in your needle," she advised Clara gently. "It might tangle." Josefina grinned. "Remember, Clara?" she said. "Mamá used to say, 'If you make your thread too long, the devil will catch on to the end of it.'"

5   All the sisters smiled and nodded, and Tía Dolores said, "I remember your mamá saying that to me when we were young girls learning to sew!"

6   Tía Dolores was smiling. But Josefina saw that her eyes were sad, and she knew that Tía Dolores was missing Mamá. Tía Dolores was Mamá's sister. Mamá had died more than a year ago. Josefina and her sisters thought of Mamá every day, with longing and love. The girls tried to do their chores the way Mamá had taught them. They tried to be as respectful, hard-working, and obedient as she would have wished them to be. Every day, they recalled her wise and funny sayings and songs. And every day, they remembered her in their prayers.

7   The first year after Mamá's death, the four girls had struggled to run the household. Then, at the end of the summer, Tía Dolores had come to visit. She was on her way home to Santa Fe from Mexico City, where she had been living for ten years. During her visit, the girls realized how much they needed someone like her — to help them and teach them as

> Mamá used to do. Tía Dolores kindly agreed to come live on the *rancho* for a while. She went to Santa Fe to see her parents for a month. But she kept her promise and returned to the *rancho* with her servant Teresita to help with the harvest. Tía Dolores had been back for two weeks now, and Josefina was glad.

1. Where does this scene take place?

   A In a sewing class
   B In the *sala* of an *adobe* house
   C In a city market
   D In a school in New Mexico

2. The fireplace is important to the story because it —

   A represents Josefina's mother to the young girls
   B almost burns Josefina
   C gives the sisters warmth and brightness on a dreary day
   D is used by Tía Dolores to cook family meals

3. How do the four sisters feel about Tía Dolores?

   A They resent their aunt's interference in their lives.
   B They want their aunt to move to Mexico City.
   C They are happy to have their aunt's help after their mother's death.
   D They, dislike their aunt trying to replace their mother.

4. What is the main problem in the story?

   A The family has to adjust to the mother's death.
   B It is difficult for them to obtain clothing.
   C There is not enough food from the harvest.
   D The sisters resent the aunt for coming to live with them.

5. Which of the following events took place first?

   A Tía Dolores gave the four sisters material to make dresses.
   B Josefina's mother died.
   C Tía Dolores visited the family on her way home.
   D Josefina finished her dress.

6. Why did Tía Dolores come for a visit at the end of the summer?

   A She wanted to see her sister's grave.
   B She was on her way home from Mexico City.
   C She knew her sister's family needed her help.
   D She wanted to experience life on a *rancho*.

CHAPTER 7

UNDERSTANDING HOW A READING WORKS

Some questions on the **TAKS Grade 4 in Reading** will test your understanding of how a story or an informational reading works — how its different parts fit together to create an impression on the reader. These questions may ask you about:

- Relationships among ideas and details in the reading
- The author's purpose or viewpoint
- Logical consistency of the reading
- Graphic organizers and outlines based on the reading

Let's begin by examining an informational reading. The selection below was written when basketball was celebrating its 100th birthday. It will provide a basis for the sample questions in this chapter.

CHILD LIFE
The Children's Own Magazine

April, May 2000   Vol. 7, Number 5

HAPPY BIRTHDAY, BASKETBALL!
by Charles Davis

1   It was the summer of 1891. Born in Canada in 1861, James Naismith had just become an instructor at the YMCA Training School in Springfield, Massachusetts. At that time, students played football in the fall and baseball in the spring. There were no winter sports. During winter

CONTINUED →

months students at the YMCA were required to do one hour of exercising each day. He had been given a challenge by his boss: to invent a new game. It had to be easy to learn and easy to play indoors during the winter. The game couldn't be rough or dangerous. Most important, it had to be fun and played to the highest standards of good sportsmanship.

2   At first, James tried taking outdoor games the students knew and bringing them indoors. But indoor rugby and soccer were too rough to play in a small gym. People could get hurt. When his students played lacrosse in the gym, they broke the windows. With only a day left before he had to report the new game to his boss, James still hadn't come up with the right game.

3   So he started thinking. Why not take parts from different games and make a new one? From soccer he chose the large ball. From lacrosse, he took the idea of a goal.

4   He decided to put the goal up high so it could not easily be defended. From football came the idea of passing the ball to move it down the court.

5   As he slept that night, he dreamed of the new game. The next morning, he wrote down thirteen rules. Then he went to look for something to use as goals.

James Naismith and his wife stand next to the peach baskets first used as the game's goals.

6   He asked building repairman Pop Stebbins for two boxes, but Pop couldn't find any. "I have two peach baskets in the storeroom. Will they do?" Pop said. James took the baskets and tacked them to the jogging track along the gym's ten-foot-high balcony.

7   As the students entered the gym, James explained the rules to them. Then the world's first basketball game got under way. It was a little confusing at first. Nobody really knew the rules yet. When the game was over, the score was 1 to 0. All the students could talk about was how much fun the new game was. They decided it needed a name.

CONTINUED

8 "How about Naismith ball?" young Frank Mahan suggested to James. "You invented it, it should have your name." James laughed, saying nobody would play a game called "Naismith ball." Frank responded, "How about basketball?" James agreed.

9 In the years following that game, basketball has changed in many ways. Bouncing the ball, or "dribbling," was added as another way to move the ball down the court. Peach baskets were replaced with metal baskets, but they still didn't have open bottoms until 1912.

10 Soon the game became the most popular activity at the YMCA. Today, it's one of the world's favorite games. James Naismith died in 1939 at age 78. He would be pleased to see modern players soar through the air for a jam or thread a pass through the lane. But he'd be even happier to see them shaking hands as friends when the game ended.

The team that played the first game of basketball at the YMCA Training School. Naismith is in a business suit.

RELATIONSHIPS AMONG IDEAS AND DETAILS

Some questions will ask about relationships among ideas and details. These questions will test your understanding of the *sequence of events, cause-and-effect relationships,* and your ability to *compare ideas and details* in a reading. You have already learned how to answer *sequence* and *cause-and-effect questions* in the last chapter. These same kinds of questions can be asked about events in an informational reading as well as events in a story. For example, look at the following questions about "Happy Birthday, Basketball!"

1. Which of these events in the history of basketball took place last?

   A Peach baskets were replaced by metal ones.
   B The baskets were given open bottoms.
   C Dribbling the ball was added to the game.
   D The game was named basketball.

2. Why did James Naismith invent the game of basketball?

   A He developed the game because he was bored.
   B His boss challenged him to invent a new game.
   C He disliked the winter and wanted to find a game played indoors.
   D His main job at the YMCA was to create new sports games.

You may recognize these two types of questions from your earlier review of story questions. **Question 1** is a *sequence question,* and **question 2** is a *cause-and-effect question.* To answer these questions, you should take the same steps as you would for questions about stories.

★ Find the part of the selection where the events in the question are discussed.

★ Then identify the correct *sequence, cause* or *effect* needed to answer the question.

Compare-and-contrast questions will ask you to compare two or more characters, persons, places, or things. Usually, the question will focus on how the items are alike or different.

3. Based on the article, what do the games of basketball and football have in common?

   A Both use baskets as goals.
   B Both require dribbling a ball.
   C Both allow the player with the ball to be tackled.
   D Both permit passing the ball to other team members.

Sometimes it helps to make a **Venn diagram** to answer a *compare-and-contrast question.* To create one, draw two overlapping circles, ovals, or boxes. Write the characteristics common to the items you are comparing in the overlapping section. Put other characteristics or information unique to each item in the other part of each circle or other shape. For example:

FOOTBALL   **BASKETBALL**

- ball must cross over a goal line
- usually played outdoors

- ball can be passed to other teammates

- ball must pass through a basket
- usually played indoors

Question 3 on the previous page asked how these two sports are alike. The Venn diagram above shows that what these two sports have in common is the passing of the ball to other teammates. Therefore, which is the correct answer?

To answer a *compare-and-contrast question*, take the following steps:

UNLOCKING THE ANSWER

First, read the question to determine if the question is looking for similarities or differences.

Next, return to the reading to find the items you need to compare. It may help to create a Venn diagram listing information about both items being compared or contrasted.

Finally, answer the question based on the information you find:

- If the question asks for similarities, pick the answer that describes both items.

- If the question asks for differences, pick a choice that tells what is found in one of the items and not in the other.

AN AUTHOR'S PURPOSE OR VIEWPOINT

Some questions may ask about an author's purpose or viewpoint. Authors generally have one of the following purposes in mind when they write:

★ **To Inform.** Informational readings — such as articles about history or science — are usually written to provide readers with information.

★ **To Entertain.** Some reading selections are written to entertain readers. Stories with interesting characters and lively plots are fun to read.

★ **To Persuade.** Some authors write to persuade readers to form a particular opinion or to take a particular action.

★ **To Express Feelings.** Some authors write to express their deepest feelings or ideas about a topic.

A question dealing with an author's purpose or viewpoint might appear as:

4 The author probably wrote "Happy Birthday, Basketball!" to —

   A inform readers how basketball was created
   B entertain readers with amusing stories about James Naismith
   C persuade readers to play the game of basketball
   D express his personal feelings about indoor sports

To answer questions identifying the author's purpose, do the following:

UNLOCKING THE ANSWER

⚷ **First**, read the selection for clues to see if it is informational, entertaining, persuasive, or expressive.

⚷ **Next**, look for the answer choice that best describes the entire selection. Answers will often include specific information about the reading. Avoid answers that only describe one part of the selection. In question 4 above, although there are some amusing stories about Naismith, this answer does not best describe the author's overall purpose in writing the article.

⚷ **Finally**, select the answer choice that best identifies the author's purpose.

Questions about an author's *viewpoint* will usually ask how the author's attitude toward the subject influences what he or she writes. For example:

5 How do the author's views in "Happy Birthday, Basketball!" influence the way he describes James Naismith?

   A He shows Naismith as someone who was always happy.
   B He describes Naismith as creative and imaginative.
   C He portrays Naismith as someone with foolish ideas.
   D He criticizes Naismith for his lack of feelings.

UNLOCKING THE ANSWER

First, review the selection to determine the author's point of view:

- Does the author like what he or she describes?
- Does the author sympathize with any of the characters?
- Is the author happy, disappointed, shocked, or angry about what he or she is writing about?

Next, think about how the author's attitude influences what he or she writes. For example, if a writer thinks that a person is bad, the author may use negative words to describe the person or what the person has done.

Finally, pick the answer that identifies the author's viewpoint.

LOGICAL CONSISTENCY

Another type of question tests your ability to tell whether the events in a story or informational reading are logical and make sense. These questions focus on whether the characters in a story behave in the way we expect people to behave. For example, look at the following question:

6 From what the reader learns about James Naismith, which statement would **NOT** be reasonable?

   A Naismith invented a protective helmet for football players.
   B Naismith excelled at sports as a young man.
   C Naismith never played any outdoor sports.
   D Naismith became the head of physical education at a university.

To answer a question dealing with the logical consistency of a reading, take these steps:

UNLOCKING THE ANSWER

🗝 **First**, read the question carefully. Often it will ask you about an event or character in the reading selection.

🗝 **Next**, review the selection to get a general sense of the character or event identified in the question:

- If the question asks which statement would be most *unreasonable*, pick the answer choice that would not be true of the character or event, based on what you have learned in the reading. For example, choice **C** would probably not be true, since Naismith knew about many outdoor games like rugby and soccer, and he even tried to have them played indoors.

- If the question asks what is *consistent* or *reasonable*, select the answer most in keeping with the way a character behaves or an event occurs in the selection. In this example, choices **A**, **B**, and **D** are all consistent with Naismith's character as a resourceful sportsman and teacher. In fact, all three sentences are true.

🗝 **Finally**, select the best answer choice.

SHOWING INFORMATION IN DIFFERENT WAYS: GRAPHIC ORGANIZERS & OUTLINES

Some questions on the test will ask you to show information from a reading in different ways. For example, you might be asked to complete:

- A graphic organizer, such as a web or Venn diagram
- A timeline or sequence map
- An outline

GRAPHIC ORGANIZERS

A **graphic organizer** presents information in a visual form. For example, a **web** places a topic or main idea at its center and surrounds it with supporting facts and details. This is useful for describing an important idea, character, or event. The main idea and supporting facts can be placed in circles, ovals, squares, or any other shape. A question about a web will ask you to complete the missing part of a web about a character, the setting, or some other part of the reading. For example, look at the question below:

7 Look at the following diagram, which shows information from the article:

Which of these belongs in the empty box?

A Players were tackled
B Baskets with open bottoms
C The ball is dribbled
D A ten-foot high goal

POINTING THE WAY

➡ Reread the selection. What details does it give you about the first basketball game as it was played in 1891? _____

➡ Which answer choice identifies information about the first basketball game that is not already listed in the three boxes in the web map? _____

A **Venn diagram,** which you learned about earlier in this chapter, is another form of graphic organizer. A **cause-and-effect graphic organizer** lists causes and effects in separate boxes or circles, with arrows showing their relationship.

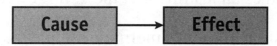

Questions about these kinds of diagrams also usually ask you to complete a missing section, based on information from the reading.

TIMELINES AND SEQUENCE MAPS

A **timeline** is a line showing times or dates, listed in the order they happened, with dates identified along the line:

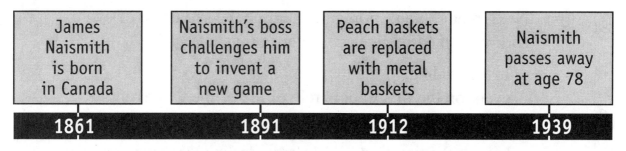

A **sequence map** is made up of a series of boxes or circles, usually linked by arrows or lines. Each box or circle represents an event in the story or informational reading. The sequence map shows how these events are connected and how things move from one event to the next. Unlike a timeline, a sequence map often does not have a specific set of dates. A question about a timeline or sequence map will usually ask you to identify a missing event. For example, look at the question that follows based on "Happy Birthday, Basketball!"

8 Look at the following diagram, which shows information from the article.

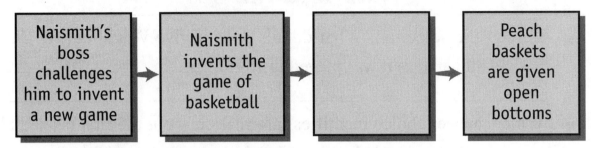

Which of these best completes the diagram?

A Players are permitted to pass the ball down the court
B Naismith tries playing rugby indoors
C Dribbling the basketball is introduced
D Naismith becomes an instructor at the YMCA school

Remember, a question about a timeline or sequence map is just like any other *sequence question* about a reading. To answer this type of question:

UNLOCKING THE ANSWER

- **First**, read through the selection to make sure you know the main events it describes.
- **Next**, read the question and examine the sequence of events shown on the timeline or sequence map.
  - In the reading, locate the event that comes before the missing event on the timeline. Circle or underline that event.
  - Then, in the reading find the event that follows the blank box on the timeline. Circle or underline this event as well.
  - Reread the sentences between the events you marked.
- **Finally**, find a choice that matches one of the events between the two you marked. That choice should be the correct answer.

Sometimes authors do not present events in a story in the same order that they are supposed to have happened. For example, a character in a story may remember an event that happened earlier in the past. Keep such special techniques in mind when putting events into a timeline or sequence map.

OUTLINES

An **outline** is almost like a skeleton. It shows the bare bones of a reading. Outlines show the main ideas and details of a reading and how they are connected. Like summaries, they leave out the less important details. People often use Roman numerals (I, II, III), letters (A, B,C) and Arabic numerals (1, 2, 3) to make an outline. An *outline question* will provide an unfinished outline and ask you to identify what is missing.

Let's look at an *outline question* based on "Happy Birthday, Basketball!":

9 Read the portion of an outline below.

> ### THE DEVELOPMENT OF BASKETBALL
> I. How basketball was invented
>   A. Naismith took parts of different games
>   1. Lacrosse: a goal
>   2. Football: passing the ball
>   3. Soccer: a large ball
>   B. Naismith added new features to the game
>   1. _____
>   2. Peach baskets used as goals
> II. How basketball has changed since it was invented
>   A. Dribbling the ball was added
>   B. Open bottoms added to baskets

Based on the article, which of the following best fits in the blank?

A Naismith was challenged to invent a new game
B Metal baskets were used
C Rugby was too dangerous indoors
D Goals were placed ten feet high

> In this question, the outline traces the development of basketball. The two major divisions of the outline are facts about the invention of basketball and facts about the later development of the sport. The missing subheading of the outline is under subheading B, "Naismith added new features to the game." These new features are in addition to those Naismith borrowed from other games. Which answer choice correctly identifies a feature of the first basketball game that Naismith did not take from another game?

To answer a question about an outline, take the following steps:

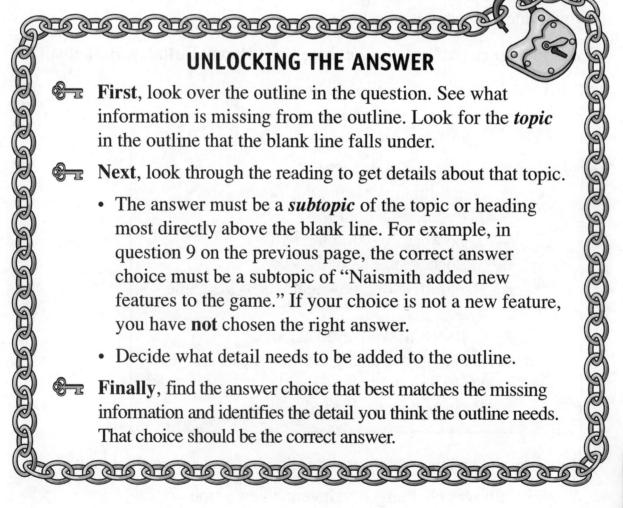

UNLOCKING THE ANSWER

- **First**, look over the outline in the question. See what information is missing from the outline. Look for the *topic* in the outline that the blank line falls under.

- **Next**, look through the reading to get details about that topic.

  - The answer must be a *subtopic* of the topic or heading most directly above the blank line. For example, in question 9 on the previous page, the correct answer choice must be a subtopic of "Naismith added new features to the game." If your choice is not a new feature, you have **not** chosen the right answer.

  - Decide what detail needs to be added to the outline.

- **Finally**, find the answer choice that best matches the missing information and identifies the detail you think the outline needs. That choice should be the correct answer.

CHAPTER 8

GOING BEYOND THE READING

Some of the questions on the **TAKS Grade 4 in Reading** will test your ability to go beyond a basic understanding of the reading and to make connections with what you already know. These questions may ask you:

- To draw conclusions from what you read
- To make predictions
- To support ideas with evidence from the reading
- To recognize how authors organize information
- To separate fact from opinion

In this chapter, you will learn how to answer multiple-choice questions that ask you to go beyond the reading. First, read the following story about a girl, her neighbor, and her "seeing-eye dog." This story will provide a basis for the practice questions appearing in this chapter.

Highlights for Children
A MAGAZINE FOR CHILDREN

September, 2001 Volume 56, Number 9

The Mystery of the Unfriendly Neighbor
By Diane Burns

1   For courage, my fingers cling to the harness on Chó's broad back as we pass my neighbor's fence. Walking by Mr. Groll's yard is the best part of our morning walk ... and also the worst.

CONTINUED

2 It is the best part because the roses talk to us. "Good morning, Chó," whisper the rose scents to my guide dog's nose. Other roses shout to me, "Hello, Mai!" with a smell that bursts bold as firecrackers. Now comes the worst part — the unfriendly shape nearby that shades us: Mr. Groll. As usual, friendly Chó thumps her tail. But Chó is just a dog; how can she know that this neighbor does not like me at all?

3 "Hello, Mr. Groll." I greet him as I do every morning. And like every other morning, he does not answer me. But I know he's there, watching behind his fence. He sounds out of breath, and the creaky gate swings nervously in his hand.

4 Maybe he's afraid of me because I'm blind. Disabilities scare grown-ups sometimes. Then I remember: yesterday I heard him playing checkers with my friend Jimmy, who's in a wheelchair. Chó and I march on, and my thoughts keep step. Why does Mr. Groll ignore me? He likes roses. I like roses. Why can't two people who like roses like each other? It's a mystery to me.

5 Chó and I stop for a moment near the rosebushes while I think. Papa has told me that some folks do not like people from faraway places. Does this solve the mystery? Maybe Mr. Groll does not like Vietnamese neighbors. No, that can't be it. Every Saturday Mr. Groll and my big brother, Lien, help each other with yard work. They are friends. Well, then, I wonder, why won't he talk to *me*?

6 The toe of my shoe scuffs the sidewalk, and I think, maybe he doesn't like girls. The sidewalk hums beneath my feet as a skateboard zooms by. "Hello, Mai and Chó!" Jana hollers. "Hi, Mr. Groll."

CONTINUED

7 I wait. If Mr. Groll ignores Jana, then the mystery is solved. But his voice calls out, "Hello, Jana!" The sound of it twists my heart. Now I know something I didn't know before: some people who can see can be blind. Sometimes, their hearts don't see any better than my eyes do. And I also know that unfriendly Mr. Groll likes Jimmy. And Lien. And Jana. But not me and Chó.

8 Me and Chó! Maybe I know why Mr. Groll doesn't talk to me! "Down," I command, releasing Chó's harness as she flops to the ground. I attach her harness to a post, and feel my way along the fence.

9 The gate squeaks open. "Mai! Be careful!" Mr. Groll's startled voice steadies my courage while his hand steadies my elbow. "You can solve my mystery," I stammer. I take a deep breath. "It isn't because I'm blind that you don't like me. Or because I am a girl from Vietnam." I sigh. "It's Chó who scares you when we walk by. That's why you are shaking even now.'

10 His large voice shrinks. "I like you, Mai. And Chó, too. But

up close, Chó scares my words away." His breath sounds thin. "A German shepherd is a very big dog," he says in a voice that tells me he thinks I will laugh at him. But being scared isn't funny. I have learned that myself. So I tell him, "Your fear of Chó may be big, but friendship is bigger. We will help. Come with me."

11 I hear a smile in Mr. Groll's voice. "OK," he says, "I trust you, my friend." Friend, he called me. We are friends! I lead him back to Chó, and tell Mr. Groll how gentle Chó is. Then I take his hand and guide it to Chó's head. Hesitantly, Mr. Groll pets Chó's ears. Friendly Chó thumps her tail. And now that the mystery is solved, our new friendship can begin.

DRAWING CONCLUSIONS

Some questions on the test may ask you to **draw conclusions** from details in a story or informational reading. A *conclusion* is a general principle or judgment you can make based on details in the reading. To answer a *conclusion question,* you'll need two things — your "thinking hat" and an ability to reason.

Conclusion questions really stretch your ability to figure things out. In these kinds of questions, the answer will *not* be found directly in the reading. Instead, like a good detective, you need to look carefully at "clues" in the reading. These details or "clues" will point to the correct answer choice.

To see how this works, pretend that you have an older sister. She and her friend have been playing softball in front of your house. Suddenly, the front doorbell rings. You open the door and your next door neighbor is standing there, holding a softball in his hand. He says the windshield on his car has been broken.

As you can see, *drawing a conclusion* requires going beyond what is written. You have to consider details in the reading and see where they point to. No one told you that your sister and her friend broke the car windshield. However, you can probably conclude that this is what happened.

A **theme** is a special kind of conclusion. It is a general message that a story often has a lesson to teach.

Now let's look at a *conclusion question* about the story you just read.

1   From the information in the story, the reader can conclude that —

   A   Mr. Groll does not like people with disabilities.
   B   Mr. Groll does not like people from Vietnam.
   C   Mr. Groll is a friendly person.
   D   Mr. Groll owns a large dog.

From information in the story, choices **A** and **B** can quickly be eliminated. Mai thinks Mr. Groll dislikes people with disabilities, but recalls that he plays with Jimmy, who is in a wheelchair. She also thinks Mr. Groll does not like Vietnamese people, but remembers he helps Lien, her brother. In paragraph 10, we learn that Mr. Groll is scared of large dogs like German shepherds. So it is reasonable to conclude that he does not own one, eliminating choice **D**. We can conclude that Mr. Groll is friendly — he is friends with Jimmy, Lien, Jana, and even Mai when she approaches him without her dog. Therefore, choice **C** is the correct answer.

To answer a conclusion question, you should take the following steps:

UNLOCKING THE ANSWER

- **First**, read the question carefully. Does it ask you to draw a conclusion from the whole passage or just a section of it?

- **Next**, look at the answer choices. Eliminate any choices that you know are incorrect. These are conclusions that cannot logically be drawn from details in the reading.

- **Finally**, look back at the reading to see which of the remaining choices is correct. Do details in the reading lead you to any of the conclusions listed in the answer choices? Choose the best one.

Now you try answering a *conclusion question* based on the same story.

2 What can the reader tell about Mai's dog, Chó, from reading this story?

   A Chó does not like the smell of roses.
   B Chó is afraid of Mr. Groll.
   C Chó is a very obedient dog.
   D Chó is still only a puppy.

PREDICTION QUESTIONS

When you read, try to predict what will happen next. As you continue reading, see if some of your predictions come true. Even when the story or informational reading reaches an end, you can try to predict what will happen next.

Prediction questions test your ability to apply what you have learned from the reading to new situations. *Prediction questions* might appear as:

> What is likely to happen next in the reading?

> What is a character from the story likely to do in the future?

For example, look at the following *prediction question*:

3 How is Mr. Groll likely to change in the future?

   A He will give up planting roses.   **C** He will say hello to Mai.
   B He will stop playing with Jimmy.   **D** He will buy a large dog.

> From the reading, we learn that Mr. Groll is afraid of Mai's dog. However, Mai guides Mr. Groll's hand across Chó to show how gentle her dog is. Based on this, how do you think Mr. Groll might change in the future?

To answer a *prediction question,* here is what you should do:

UNLOCKING THE ANSWER

- **First**, think about what you have learned in the reading.

- **Next**, use what you have learned to predict what is likely to happen in a new or different situation. The answer must be in keeping with information in the story. For example, choice **D** is unlikely since Mr. Groll still has a strong fear of large dogs. However, because of the actions of Mai, he has become less afraid of Chó and will probably greet Mai in the future.

- **Finally**, select the answer choice closest to your prediction.

Now you try to answer a *prediction question:*

4 If the story were to continue, what would be most likely to happen next?

   A Mai's father would scold Mr. Groll for ignoring his daughter.
   B Mr. Groll would move from the neighborhood.
   C Mai and Mr. Groll would become better friends.
   D Mai would get a new guide dog to lead her.

HOW THE READING IS ORGANIZED

Authors organize their writing in different ways, based on what they want to say. You have already learned about some of these ways of organizing a reading selection in previous chapters:

> ★ **Sequencing** — telling about a series of events in the order in which they happened.
> ★ **Description** — describing the qualities of a person, place, or thing.
> ★ **Compare / Contrast** — telling how two or more items are alike or different.
> ★ **Cause / Effect** — giving the causes of an event, describing the event, and telling the effects of that event.
> ★ **Problem / Solution** — describing a problem and telling about its possible solution.

Some questions may ask you how information in a reading selection is organized. For example, look at the following question about "The Mystery of the Unfriendly Neighbor."

5 The author organizes paragraphs 4 through 8 of the story by —

   A telling Mai's thoughts as she tries to figure out why Mr. Groll dislikes her
   B describing the flowers that Mai and Mr. Groll both like
   C explaining why blind people like Mai need a guide dog
   D listing the problems that people with disabilities sometimes face in society.

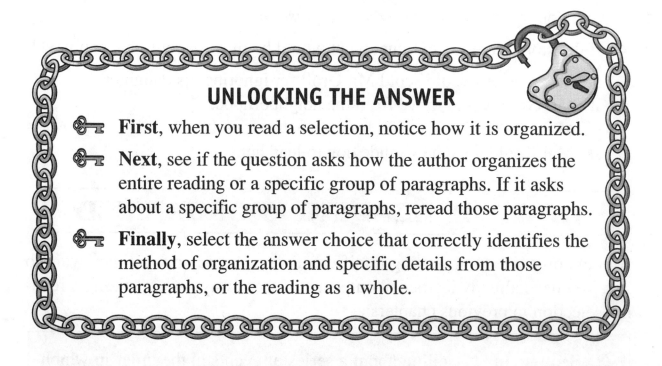

UNLOCKING THE ANSWER

- **First**, when you read a selection, notice how it is organized.
- **Next**, see if the question asks how the author organizes the entire reading or a specific group of paragraphs. If it asks about a specific group of paragraphs, reread those paragraphs.
- **Finally**, select the answer choice that correctly identifies the method of organization and specific details from those paragraphs, or the reading as a whole.

SUPPORTING IDEAS ABOUT A READING WITH SPECIFIC EXAMPLES

Another type of question asks you to support an idea or view of the reading with specific evidence from it. This kind of question tests your ability to connect general statements to details in the reading. Look at the following example:

6 Which sentence shows that Mai thinks Mr. Groll does not like her?

   A *It is the best part because the roses talk to us.*

   B *Now comes the worst part – the unfriendly shape nearby that shades us: Mr. Groll.*

   C *He sounds out of breath, and the creaky gate swings nervously in his hand.*

   D *"But up close, Chó scares my words away."*

Think of this kind of question as asking you to pretend you are a lawyer in court. You tell the jury: "Ladies and gentlemen, Mai thinks that Mr. Groll does not like her!" However, your opinion is not enough to persuade the jury. You have to give information from the story to prove your statement.

To answer a question asking you to support a statement or view with information from the reading, take the following steps:

> **UNLOCKING THE ANSWER**
>
> - **First**, read the question carefully, making sure you understand what it says. Does the question ask you to find facts, examples, or specific sentences? Briefly look at the answer choices. Actual sentences will usually appear in *italics*. When actual sentences are used, you must decide which sentence best supports the view stated in the question.
>
> - **Next**, if you cannot answer the question just by reading the answer choices, locate the section of the reading that has information about the question. In question 7, you would have to reread the story until you came to paragraph 2. Here you will find evidence that Mai believes Mr. Groll does not like her.
>
> - **Finally**, go back to the answer choices. Based on the information you found in the selection, which answer choice best supports the statement in the question?

Now, let's practice answering a question asking you to support a statement with specific information.

7. Which sentence in the story shows that Mai thinks Mr. Groll may dislike foreigners?

   A *Disabilities scare grown-ups sometimes.*
   B *Papa has told me that some folks do not like people from faraway places.*
   C *Every Saturday, Mr. Groll and my big brother, Lien, help each other with yard work.*
   D *Now I know something I didn't know before: some people who can see can be blind.*

FACT-AND-OPINION QUESTIONS

Do you know the difference between a **fact** and an **opinion?** Some questions may ask you to identify a fact or an opinion. On the **TAKS Grade 4 in Reading,** *fact-and-opinion questions* will only be asked about informational readings that try to persuade their readers.

FACT

A **fact** is a statement that can be shown to be correct or true. "The table is red" is a statement of fact. People can look at the table to see if it is red. Other facts can be checked by using other sources. Suppose someone tells you that there was a fire yesterday at 42 Maple Lane. You can look in the newspaper, call the fire department, or even visit Maple Lane to check if there really was a fire.

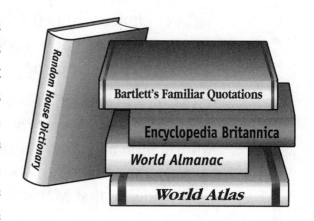

OPINION

An **opinion** is a statement of personal feelings or beliefs. Words such *as think, feel, probably,* and *believe* often show that a statement is an opinion. This statement is an opinion: "I believe Sam Houston was the greatest governor of Texas." No one can prove Houston was our greatest governor. The statement just tells us the writer's personal belief.

Writers often make statements that look like facts even though they are actually opinions. For example, "Our soap cleans the best." Writers do this to sound more convincing. Ask yourself: Can this be checked, or is it an expression of the writer's beliefs?

Let's practice answering a *fact-and-opinion question*. Read the letter below to the Director of the Museum of Natural Science in Houston about a possible exhibit.

Director, Museum of Natural Science
1 Hermann Circle
Houston, Texas

Dear Director,
    I have recently read that the Museum of Natural Science is thinking about having a special exhibit on Albert Einstein. I am writing to say that I think this would be an excellent idea.

    Einstein's theories changed many of our scientific ideas. He developed the "theory of relativity." This theory states that time and space are related. How fast time passes is based on how fast something moves. At the speed of light, Einstein said, time stands still. Einstein also said that things could be changed into immense amounts of energy. All this may seem very strange, but experiments have shown that Einstein was right. His theories led to the development of the atomic bomb and nuclear energy.

    As one of the greatest scientist of all times, Einstein surely deserves to have a special exhibit at the Houston museum. The exhibit could focus on explaining his "theory of relativity" and all the wonderful discoveries and inventions this theory has led to.

                             Sincerely,
                               Cedric Williams

Now that you have finished reading this letter, answer the question that follows.

8 Which of the following is an opinion?

   A *Einstein's theories changed many of our scientific ideas.*
   B *This theory states that time and space are related.*
   C *At the speed of light, Einstein said, time stands still.*
   D *As one of the greatest scientists of all times, Einstein surely deserves to have a special exhibit at the Houston museum.*

CHAPTER 9

QUESTIONS ABOUT PAIRED READINGS

On the **TAKS Grade 4 in Reading** you may find **paired readings** — two readings on a related topic or theme. The two selections together will be about as long as other single selections on the test. The questions that follow the paired readings will be in three sections: those on the *first reading,* those on the *second reading,* and those on **both readings.**

The questions on individual readings will be the same as those you have learned about in earlier chapters. This chapter looks at the special types of questions that may be asked about both selections. These questions may ask:

| How are the readings similar? | How are the readings different? | How do the readings compare in their approach, organization or development? |

These questions are similar to other *compare-and-contrast questions,* except that they ask you to compare one reading selection with another. Let's begin by examining two paired readings typical of those on the actual test.

THE EMPEROR AND THE PEASANT BOY

1   Once there was an emperor who liked to disguise himself and travel among his people to discover their true opinions and feelings. One day, the emperor dressed in disguise and went into the countryside. During his walk, he came upon a poor young boy gathering twigs for his family.

CONTINUED

2 "You hardly have enough twigs to build a fire," the emperor told the boy. "Why not collect more twigs from the royal forest across the road?"

3 The boy spoke back to the stranger: "Kind traveler, you are not from these parts. If you were, you would know that the forest belongs to the emperor. It is forbidden for anyone to enter the royal forest."

4 "Surely," the emperor replied, "no one would know if you went there. Your emperor must be cruel to allow twigs to lie in the forest while his people go cold without a fire."

5 "I agree with you that the law is unjust," the boy said, "but the law is the law. I will not disobey it." He then walked away carrying his small bundle of twigs.

6 One week later, the boy and his family were called to the palace. When they arrived, they were brought to the emperor's throne room. There, the boy recognized the stranger, sitting on the throne and wearing a crown.

7 "Fear not," said the emperor, "you've done nothing wrong. You refused to steal when you had the chance, and you insisted on obeying your emperor's law. I just wanted to meet the parents who raised such an honest child." A servant brought in a huge chest filled with gold, which the emperor gave to the peasant boy's family.

8 The emperor then said, "I've decided to change the law governing the royal forest. You were right, young man. The law is unjust and unfair. From now on, all the people in my kingdom can use the forest to meet their needs. Your honesty, young man, has truly touched my heart."

MERCURY AND THE WOODCUTTER

1 A poor woodcutter was once cutting down a tree near a lake. It was late, and he had been working since sunrise. His strokes were not as sure as they had been in the morning. The axe flew out of his hands and landed in the lake.

2 The axe was all the poor woodcutter owned for making a living. As he stood weeping, the god Mercury appeared and asked why he was crying. After the woodcutter related what had happened, Mercury dived into the lake. He soon returned to the surface holding a wonderful golden axe. "Is this your axe?" Mercury asked.

3 "No," answered the woodcutter, "that's not mine." Mercury laid the axe down and jumped back into the lake. This time he came up with an axe made of silver, but the woodcutter declared his axe was just an ordinary one with a wooden handle.

4 Mercury dived into the lake a third time. When he came out of the water, Mercury held the very axe that had been lost. The woodcutter was happy his axe had been found. Mercury was greatly pleased with the woodcutter's honesty.

5 "I admire your honesty," he said, " and as a reward, you may have all three axes — the gold and the silver as well as your own." The happy woodcutter returned home to his family with his new treasure.

6 Soon the woodcutter's good fortune was known to all the village. Several woodcutters in the village believed that they could easily win the same good fortune. They hurried into the woods and hid their axes in the bushes, pretending to have lost them. Then they wept and called on Mercury to help them.

CONTINUED

> **7** Indeed, Mercury did appear. To each woodcutter, Mercury showed an axe of gold, and each one claimed it to be the one he had lost. But Mercury did not give them the golden axe. Instead, he gave each one of them a hard whack over the head with the golden axe and sent them fleeing home.
>
> **8** When they returned the next day to retrieve their own axes, they were nowhere to be found.

HOW THE READINGS ARE SIMILAR

Paired readings will always be about a common theme or topic. Sometimes, the same story might even be told twice — each time from the point of view of a different character in the story. When you read paired readings, think about the link between them. Some test questions may ask you about their common theme, or about anything else the two reading selections may have in common.

These questions could ask about similarities in theme, plot, setting, or the characteristics of the characters. For example, a question might appear as:

1. How are the peasant boy and the first woodcutter similar?

   A Both are loyal subjects of the emperor.
   B Both have gone into a royal forest.
   C Both show qualities of honesty.
   D Both work with wooden axes.

> This question asks what the peasant boy and the first woodcutter have in common. Both stories are about characters trying to get wood. The peasant boy is collecting twigs, while the woodcutter is cutting a tree with his axe. Because the peasant boy has no axe, choice **D** is wrong. Since the peasant boy refuses to go into the royal forest and the second story has no royal forest, choice **B** is also wrong. There is no emperor in the second story, so choice **A** must also be wrong. Only choice **C** clearly applies to both characters. In fact, honesty is the common theme that unites the two selections.

Very often, a question asking about similarities will ask about the common theme linking the two selections. To answer a question about similarities, take the following steps:

UNLOCKING THE ANSWER

- **First**, see what the question focuses on.
  - Does it ask about particular characters, events, or places in the two selections?
  - Does it ask about the selections' common topic or theme?

- If the question asks about the common theme linking the two selections, think about each selection as a whole.
  - What is its message?
  - How is the message of the first reading similar to that of the second? Look at the answer choices and pick the one that best identifies the common theme shared by the two selections.

- If the question asks about similarities between specific characters, events, places, or objects in the two stories:
  - Review each story, especially those parts the question asks you to compare.
  - It may help you to (circle) or underline the people or things being compared. You can even make an imaginary Venn diagram in your head to help you highlight important information.
  - Look for any similarities between the two items you are comparing. Then select the answer that best identifies those similarities.

Now that you have learned about questions on similarities, put your knowledge to use by answering the following question:

2 How is the plot of "The Emperor and the Peasant Boy" similar to that of "Mercury and the Woodcutter"?

   A In both stories, a poor person refuses to lie to a god.
   B In both stories, a poor person refuses to break the law.
   C In both stories, a poor person is rewarded for his honesty.
   D In both stories, a poor person loses something he needs.

HOW THE READINGS ARE DIFFERENT

Although paired readings will have some similarities, they will also be different in some ways. A question on the differences between paired stories might ask how the two selections treat a common theme differently, or ask for differences between characters, places, events, or objects in the two selections. Look at the following questions about the paired readings in this chapter.

3 Look at the chart comparing the two stories. It shows story differences.

The Emperor and the Peasant Boy	Mercury and the Woodcutter
• A poor peasant boy is collecting twigs	• A woodcutter is chopping down a tree.
• The emperor tells the boy to take wood from the royal forest.	• The god Mercury offers the woodcutter a golden axe.
• The boy refuses to break the law by taking wood from the forest.	• _____

Which of these best completes the chart?

   A The woodcutter jumps into the lake to find his axe.
   B The woodcutter refuses to tell his wife how he got the axes.
   C The woodcutter refuses to lie by claiming the golden axe is his.
   D The woodcutter refuses to enter the emperor's royal forest.

> This question asks you to identify an important difference between the two selections. Here, you are asked to find a missing piece of a graphic organizer — a chart. Choices **A, B,** and **D** refer to events that are not found in "Mercury and the Woodcutter." Only one answer choice correctly identifies an action taken by the woodcutter in the story.

4 What is one difference between the emperor and the god Mercury?

   A Mercury rewarded honesty with riches.
   B The emperor admired honesty.
   C Mercury tempted someone to take what was not his.
   D The emperor's beliefs changed.

> In this question, you have to identify an important difference between the two selections. The answer choices all refer to actions taken by the emperor or by Mercury. For example, Choice **A** refers to an action taken by Mercury. But a similar action was also taken by the emperor when he rewarded the peasant boy's family with riches. Which of the remaining answer choices correctly identifies an action taken by one of the characters but not the other?

To answer a question asking about differences between paired readings, take the following steps:

UNLOCKING THE ANSWER

- **First**, see what the question focuses on. Just as you would do for questions about similarities, see if the question focuses on the selection as a whole or on specific characters or events.

- If the question asks about specific characters or events, go back to both readings and review all sections describing those characters or events. It may help to jot down important differences or to make an imaginary Venn diagram in your mind showing those differences.

- **Finally**, choose the answer that correctly identifies a difference between the two readings. Remember, the key is to ask: does this answer choice apply to both themes, characters or events? In answering a question on differences, the correct answer choice may apply to one reading *but not both*.

COMPARING THE APPROACH, ORGANIZATION AND DEVELOPMENT

Some questions may specifically ask how the two readings compare in their approach, organization, and development. Even though the paired readings treat a common theme, each author may approach that theme differently. For example one of the paired readings might be "An Essay on Honesty," giving the reasons why honesty is important, while the other reading might be the story "The Emperor and the Peasant Boy," which you have just read. A question could ask you to identify either a similarity or a difference between the organization and development of these two readings. Although you have not read the essay, you can probably guess the answer to this question:

5   How is the organization of "The Emperor and the Peasant Boy" different from that of "The Essay on Honesty"?

   A One selection lists reasons; the other selection tells a story.
   B One selection praises honesty; the other ignores it.
   C One selection lists reasons; the other persuades readers to be honest.
   D One selection provides facts; the other expresses feelings.

To answer this kind of question, take the following steps:

UNLOCKING THE ANSWER

- **First**, identify each type of reading and its method of organization whenever you come across paired readings on the test. Is each reading meant to inform, express, entertain, persuade or perform a mixture of these?

- **Then**, see if the question asks for *similarities* or *differences* in the approaches, plan of organization, or development of the two selections.

- **Finally**, select the answer choice that best identifies how the two readings are alike or different.

UNIT 3: A PRACTICE READING TEST

In this section, you will have an opportunity to apply the many skills you've learned to see how much you have improved. This practice test is designed to be like the real **TAKS Grade 4 in Reading.**

There are four reading selections on this test — an informational reading, a set of paired readings, and a story. Each selection or pair of readings is followed by several multiple-choice questions. At the end of each multiple-choice question, you will find the objective it is testing. The objective number is provided to help you and your teacher identify any kinds of questions you may need additional practice in answering. You may look back at the selections and questions as often as you like. If you finish the test early, spend the time checking over your work. *Good luck on this practice test!*

CHAPTER 10
A PRACTICE TAKS IN READING

Read the following selection. Then answer questions 1 through 13.

ALVIN AILEY
by Andrea Davis Pinkney

1   Alvin Ailey was born in 1931 in Rogers, Texas. As a young boy, he grew up in Navasota, Texas, where he regularly attended church with his mother. His memories of stomping feet, clapping hands, and singing along with the church choir inspired young Alvin to want to study dance.

CONTINUED

2 As a young man, Alvin moved to Los Angeles to study dance. But when Alvin arrived in Los Angeles in 1949, not everyone could take dance lessons. Alvin was African American, and in those days not many dance schools accepted black students. And almost none taught the fluid moves that Alvin liked so much — almost none but the Lester Horton Dance Theatre School, a modern dance school that welcomed students of all races.

3 Lester's door was open to anyone serious about learning to dance. And, at age eighteen, Alvin Ailey was serious, especially when he saw how Lester's dancers moved. One student danced with a butterfly's grace. Another made modern dance look easy. But Lester worked his students hard. Sometimes they danced all day.

4 After hours in the studio, droplets of sweat dotted Alvin's forehead. He tingled inside, ready to try Lester's steps once more. At first, Alvin kept time to Lester's beat and followed Lester's moves. Then Alvin's own rhythm took over, and he started creating his own steps. Alvin's <u>tempo</u> worked from his belly to his elbows, then oozed through his thighs and feet.

5 Alvin danced at Lester Horton's school almost every day. He taught the other students his special moves. In 1950, Alvin joined Lester Horton's dance company. Soon Alvin performed his own <u>choreography</u> for small audiences at Lester's studio. His dances told stories — he flung his arms to express joy. Modern dance let Alvin's imagination whirl.

6 All the while, Lester watched Alvin grow into a strong dancer and choreographer. Lester told Alvin to study and learn as much as he could about dance. He encouraged Alvin to use his memories and his African-American heritage to make dances that were unforgettable.

CONTINUED

7 Some tried to follow Alvin's moves, but even Alvin didn't know which way his body would turn next. Alvin's steps flowed from one another. His loops and spins just came to him, the way daydreams do.

8 In 1958, Alvin left Los Angeles for New York City. He was glad to be in New York. He had come to learn ballet and modern dance techniques from Martha Graham, one of the best teachers in the world.

9 Alvin took dance classes all over town, and he met dancers who showed him moves he'd never seen before. So many of the dancers he met were African American. Like Alvin, their dreams soared higher than New York's tallest skyscrapers.

10 In the late 1950s, Alvin gathered some of the dancers he'd seen in classes around the city. He chose the men and women who had just the right moves to dance to his choreography. Alvin told them he wanted to start a modern dance company that would dance to blues and gospel music — the heritage of African-American people. Nine dancers believed in Alvin's idea. This was the beginning of the Alvin Ailey American Dance Theatre.

11 On March 30, 1958, on an old wooden stage at the 92nd Street Y, Alvin and his friends opened for the first time with *Blues Suite,* dances set in a honky-tonk dance hall. Alvin's choreography depicted the blues, that weepy sadness all folks feel now and then. Alvin moved in time to the music, the same way he did when he was a boy. The audience swayed in their seats as Alvin and his company danced. When the show ended, the audience went wild with applause. They stomped and shouted. "More!"

CONTINUED

12   Taking a bow, Alvin let out a breath. He was satisfied and proud. Alvin was on his way to making it big. Word spread about him and his dancers. Newspapers hailed him. Under his leadership, the American Dance Theatre went on to receive international <u>acclaim</u>.

Use the article "Alvin Ailey" to answer questions 1–13

1 What is the article mostly about?

  A A young African American studies dance in Texas, California, and New York.

  B Alvin Ailey learns to dance with grace at the Lester Horton Dance Theatre School.

  C Alvin Ailey's *Blues Suite* opens on March 30, 1958, at the 92nd Street YMCA.

  D A young African American studies dance and forms a new dance company celebrating his heritage.

Objective 1

2 What words help the reader to understand what <u>choreography</u> means in paragraph 5?

  A *other students*
  B *small audiences*
  C *imagination whirl*
  D *his dances*

Objective 1

3 Read the meanings below for the word <u>blues</u>.

> **blues** (blooz), *plural noun*
> 1. a mood of sadness 2. a type of jazz music
> 3. copies of a manuscript about to be published
> 4. blue uniform worn by members of the U. S. Navy

Which meaning best fits the way <u>blues</u> is used in paragraph 11?

  A Meaning 1   **C** Meaning 3
  B Meaning 2   **D** Meaning 4

Objective 1

4 The author's purpose in writing this selection was to —

  A describe the birth of dance
  B persuade readers to attend a dance performance
  C explain why young people often love to dance
  D inform readers how a determined dancer rose to fame

Objective 3

5 In paragraph 4, the word <u>tempo</u> means —

A the rhythm of Alvin's movements
B the happiness Alvin feels
C the sweat on Alvin's skin
D the smoothness of his dance moves

Objective 1

6 In paragraph 11, members of the audience sway in their seats because they —

A swing to the rhythm of Alvin's new dance company
B think Alvin is on his way to making big
C dislike the music that Ailey's company is dancing to
D are uncomfortable inside an old building

Objective 3

7 Based on this selection, why were many African-American students prevented from taking dance lessons in the 1940s?

A African-American studios disliked classical music.
B Many dance schools did not admit African Americans.
C Most African-American students lacked dancing ability.
D Many African American students could not afford dance lessons.

Objective 3

8 The author organizes paragraphs 10 and 11 by —

A comparing Ailey's style of dance with other styles
B identifying a problem that Ailey faced and telling how he solved it
C telling about events in Ailey's life in the order they occurred
D recounting Ailey's innermost thoughts

Objective 4

9 In paragraph 12, the word <u>acclaim</u> means —

A criticism
B attack
C dancing
D praise

Objective 1

10 From information in the article, the reader can conclude that —

A the audience at the 92nd Street Y did not really enjoy *Blues Suite*
B Ailey's childhood experiences influenced his style of dancing
C Ailey preferred Los Angeles to New York
D Ailey disliked dancing in front of large groups

Objective 4

11 Which of the following is the best summary of the article?

A Ailey moved to New York City in 1958 to learn ballet and modern dance from Martha Graham. Then he gathered dancers he had met in classes around the city. Nine dancers joined his new dance group.

B Ailey moved from Texas to Los Angeles to study dance. Lester Horton welcomed Ailey when many dance schools refused to accept African Americans. Ailey studied hard and soon was dancing to his own rhythms. He later studied dance in New York City.

C Under Ailey, the American Dance Theatre became famous. Their first performance was in March, 1958, at the 92nd Street Y. They performed his *Blues Suite,* which was set in a dance hall.

D Ailey grew up in Texas, where he learned singing and dancing in church. He studied fluid dance moves in Los Angeles with Lester Horton. In New York City, Ailey studied and began his own dance company, which danced to blues and gospel music as he had done as a boy. *Objective 1*

12 Which sentence from the article shows that Ailey developed a natural and fluid way of dancing?

A *His memories of stomping feet, clapping hands, and singing along with the church choir inspired young Alvin to want to study dance.*

B *At first, Alvin kept time to Lester's beat and followed Lester's moves.*

C *The audience swayed in their seats as Alvin and his company danced.*

D *Alvin's tempo worked from his belly to his elbows, then oozed through his thighs and feet.* *Objective 4*

13 From information in the article, which New York City attraction would Alvin Ailey most likely have enjoyed seeing?

A A trip to the United Nations
B A cruise on the Hudson River
C The Thanksgiving Day Parade
D A visit to a Broadway musical

Objective 4

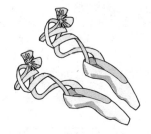

THE MISER AND HIS TREASURE

1   There once lived a <u>miser</u>. Like all misers, this man preferred to save his money rather than to spend any of it. This miser was so worried about his money that he buried his gold in a secret place in his garden. Every day the miser would dig up his treasure and count it.

2   One day a passing thief, who had been secretly watching the miser, guessed what he had buried in his garden. That night, after the miser went to bed, the thief crept into the garden. The thief dug up the treasure and ran away.

3   The next day, the miser returned again to dig up his treasure. When the miser discovered his loss, he felt destroyed. He did nothing but cry without stopping for days and days.

4   A passerby heard the sobbing miser and asked him, "What happened to you to make you cry like this?"

5   After the miser told his story, the passerby asked him, "Why didn't you keep your money in the house where you could reach it easily and use it to buy things to make your life comfortable?"

6   The miser, angered by this question, screamed in reply, "I never touched that gold. I could not bring myself to spend even one penny of it!"

7   The stranger then picked up a large stone lying on the ground and threw it into the empty hole. "If that is the case, sir," he said, "cover up that stone. It's worth as much to you as the treasure you have lost."

HARD-BOILED EGGS

A tale from Hungary retold by Tom Kovach

1 In the kingdom of Hungary there once lived a man named Janos Kadar. After years of hard work, Janos was able to pay off all his debts and have enough money left to live comfortably. So one sunny morning he set out to repay a kind innkeeper who had once helped Janos when he was poor and hungry.

2 This innkeeper was surprised to see Janos. "Good day to you," said Janos. "Ten years ago you gave me two boiled eggs when I was hungry and had no money. Today, I want to reward your kindness by paying for those eggs a hundredfold!"

3 But the ten years had changed the innkeeper from a generous man to a greedy one. He began figuring what would have happened had the two eggs hatched chicks, and had those chicks grown up and hatched more chicks, and so on. He finally concluded that Janos should give him everything he had.

4 Janos was surprised and upset that his kind gesture should be met with such greedy demands. The news of this soon spread throughout the land until the king of Hungary himself heard the story and agreed to sit in judgment of what should be done.

CONTINUED

5 As the time drew near for Janos and the innkeeper to present their cases, poor Janos grew sad. His hard-earned savings would be lost, for the king would surely decide in favor of the innkeeper.

6 One day, as he sat thinking about his bad luck, a traveling gypsy came by [*gypsies were a wandering people*]. "Why are you so sad?" the gypsy asked.

7 When Janos explained, the gypsy laughed. "Don't worry. Let me present your case, and you'll surely win." Janos agreed to let the gypsy try.

8 The day of the trial arrived, but when Janos reached the king's chamber, the gypsy was nowhere to be found. Everybody sat waiting, until finally the king grew impatient. "Janos Kadar," he said, "if the man representing you doesn't arrive in one minute, you'll have to pay the innkeeper all he asks for."

9 Just at that moment, the gypsy burst through the door. "I'm sorry for being late, Your Majesty," he said breathlessly, "but I was at home boiling corn, trying to turn it into more corn!"

10 Everyone in the king's chamber laughed. "Silly man," said the king, "how can you make more corn from boiled corn?"

11 The gypsy smiled. "Well then, how can you hatch chicks from boiled eggs?"

12 "You're right," the king said. "If the eggs were boiled, it would be impossible to hatch chicks! Janos, pay only for the two eggs you ate."

13 Janos thanked the king and gypsy traveler, paid the innkeeper, and happily went home. As for the innkeeper, because of his greed he only got paid for the two eggs, instead of the large reward Janos had first offered him.

CHAPTER 10: A PRACTICE TAKS IN READING 125

Use "The Miser and His Treasure Chest" to answer questions 14–17

14 In paragraph 1, the word <u>miser</u> means a person who —

   A is afraid to spend any money
   B enjoys making others miserable
   C invests money wisely
   D never marries

   Objective 1

15 What did the passerby mean when he said the stone was worth as much as the lost treasure?

   A The thief might one day return to steal the stone.
   B The gold had no value to the miser since he never spent it.
   C The stone was valuable to people who collect stones.
   D The thought was made of precious minerals.

   Objective 1

16 Why did the miser bury his gold in the garden?

   A He had stolen it.
   B He feared the king would demand it to pay for taxes.
   C He preferred looking at it to spending it.
   D He thought his treasure might grow.

   Objective 2

17 What lesson does this story teach us?

   A Crime does not pay.
   B It is better to give than to receive.
   C Money is the root of all evil.
   D Money only has value if it is spent.

   Objective 4

Use "Hard-Boiled Eggs" to answer questions 18–24

18 What are paragraphs 3 and 4 mostly about?

   A Janos ignores an innkeeper who helped him many years before.
   B Janos wants to repay an innkeeper who now demands too much.
   C Janos wants to give his fortune to an innkeeper who once helped him.
   D Janos wants to teach a greedy innkeeper to be generous.

   Objective 1

19 In paragraph 4, the word <u>gesture</u> means —

   A a movement of the head
   B a pointing of the hand
   C an action showing feeling
   D a joke or humorous story

   Objective 1

20 Read the meanings below for the word <u>trial</u>.

   trial (trī′ ol), *noun*
   1. act of trying something out 2. test performed on a product
   3. public examination of evidence to decide a case 4. a difficult experience that tests a person's faith.

   Which meaning best fits the way <u>trial</u> is used in paragraph 8?

   A Meaning 1
   B Meaning 2
   C Meaning 3
   D Meaning 4

   Objective 1

21 What is the main problem of the story?

   A Janos refuses to pay the innkeeper what he owes.
   B The innkeeper tries to take Janos's savings by making a false claim.
   C The gypsy needs more corn.
   D The innkeeper needs money for his family to live comfortably.

   Objective 2

22 Which of the following best describes the gypsy?

   A Greedy and selfish
   B Respected and powerful
   C Light-hearted but clever
   D Kind but foolish

   Objective 2

23 If the gypsy had not arrived when he did, the king would most probably have —

A given Janos's savings to the innkeeper
B demanded Janos's savings for himself
C sent both Janos and the innkeeper away
D punished the innkeeper for his greed

Objective 4

24 What is the best reply the innkeeper could have given to the gypsy?

A If Janos hadn't come to his inn, he never would have boiled the eggs.
B The gypsy had no right to interfere in the dispute.
C Janos owed the innkeeper money for other services.
D Boiled eggs might still hatch chicks.

Objective 4

Use both "The Miser and His Treasure" and "Hard-Boiled Eggs" to answer questions 25 and 26.

---

25 How are the miser and the innkeeper most alike?

A Both are dishonest people.
B Both have been robbed of what belongs to them.
C Both value riches above other thing.
D Both were once generous people.

Objective 3

26 Look at the chart below. It tells about story differences.

STORY DIFFERENCES

The Miser and His Treasure	Hard-Boiled Eggs
• The miser does not spend his treasure.	• The innkeeper spends his money.
• The miser is robbed of his treasure.	• Janos is able to keep his money.
• The miser does not cheat anyone.	• _____

Which statement **BEST** completes the chart?

A The innkeeper was once generous.
B The innkeeper does not trust the gypsy.
C The innkeeper is subject to the king's decision.
D The innkeeper tries to cheat Janos.

Objective 3

KILLER
by Sandy Fox

1 Killer, they called him. He stood in the field, head down, bony ribs showing. As I walked past on my way home from school, I stopped whistling. "Hey, Champion!" I called.

2 He wiggled an ear and turned his head. Last year, he'd run every time I walked by.

3 Dad said he'd killed Old Man Wiggins's son. The scar on his side was where Old Man Wiggins tried to kill him. The horse had raced off into the woods, and the old man yelled after him, "Go starve to death."

4 Must have been ten years ago, and Killer — <u>mangy</u>, bony, with matted mane (*hair*) and tail — was still alive. Dad said you call someone what you want him to be. To me, he was a champion. I pulled out some carrots. "Champion! Come get your carrots."

5 His neck bent toward me. "Come on. I won't hurt you." He didn't take a step in my direction. He'd been coming closer to the fence each afternoon, and I'd thought I was getting somewhere. I put the carrots on the ground and walked off, whistling "When the Saints Go Marching In."

CONTINUED

6 When I was little and scared, Dad taught me to whistle. I'd gotten into the habit of whistling whenever I walked by next to Champion's field. I wasn't scared or anything. I didn't even mind going home to an empty house until Dad got off work.

7 The next afternoon I passed by Champion's field again. He was standing in the same gully, with the carrots lying uneaten by the fence. "What's the matter, Champ?" His ears flickered, and his head swung around. When he lifted his back foot, I saw a barbed wire wrapped around it.

8 Trapped! He'd been standing there all night and all day. Without food or water. Dad would not be home for hours. Would he let me help him or was he really a mean killer?

9 His big brown eyes looked at me again. I dropped my backpack and wiggled through the fence. Champ tried to back up but then stood still, his ears pinned back. I swallowed, licked my lips, and began to whistle. "O when the saints …"

10 Champ's ears flipped forward. I whistled to drown out the pounding of my heart as I walked up to him. He flinched when I touched him. "It's O.K. I won't hurt you." I slid my hand down his side. I could feel him trembling, and I thought he's as scared as I am.

11 I began to whistle as I slowly slid my hand to his rump. The barbed wire dug into his leg and wrapped itself around his thigh. I'd have to hurt him to set him free. I'd have to bend close to his sharp hoofs and lean under him.

12 I looked at him and saw him looking at me. "Will you stand still for this?" I asked him. "I'm sorry, but it's going to hurt." He bobbed his head. "Good." I smiled and grabbed the rusted wire. As I tried to unwind it, the wire hit his other hind leg. He cow-kicked and I froze. If he went crazy, we could both be killed.

13 I began whistling under my breath. He put his hind leg down. I waited a minute, my hand still resting on his rump until his muscles relaxed and he let out a breath. Slowly I bent over, grabbed the wire from beneath his tail, and unwound another twist.

14 The last loop had dug into his thigh. Gently I tugged it loose. Champ flinched but stood quietly as the barb pulled off matted hair and skin.

15 "I'm sorry, Champ. I'm trying to be gentle." Blood oozed from the cut. I pulled more wire from his skin, unwinding the rusted <u>mass</u> around the tree that had anchored the wire.

16 Now that he was free, would he run, kick or bite? Champ kept his eyes on me. When I was six feet away, he lifted his back foot. I froze as he walked toward me. He blew gently in my face and sniffed my chest.

17 Slowly my hand touched his cheek. He stiffened and then relaxed. "You are a champion!" I grinned. As I walked to the fence, Champ walked beside me — limping, but walking.

Use the story "Killer" to answer questions 27–40.

27 What are paragraphs 1 through 4 mostly about?

   A A horse lived in a field since killing a boy.
   B Old Man Wiggins' son was killed by a horse.
   C A horse's ribs were starting to show.
   D A boy fed a horse some carrots.

   Objective 1

28 Read the meanings below for the word mass.

   > **mass** (mas), *noun*
   >
   > 1. a unified body of matter.
   > 2. the majority or major part of something.
   > 3. the weight of something.
   > 4. a group of something clumped together.

   Which meaning best fits the way mass is used in paragraph 15?

   A Meaning 1
   B Meaning 2
   C Meaning 3
   D Meaning 4

   Objective 1

29 In paragraph 4, the word mangy means —

   A dirty and shabby
   B clean and fresh
   C quiet and lonely
   D hungry and thirsty

   Objective 1

30 What is the main problem in the story?

   A Killer is prevented from becoming a champion race horse.
   B A horse's fear of people is interpreted as being unfriendly.
   C A boy helps an abandoned horse that may be dangerous.
   D A horse refuses to eat carrots from anyone.

   Objective 2

31 Why is it important that the story take place in an open field?

- A It shows the role of Old Man Wiggins in the story.
- B It shows that the abandoned horse is living on its own.
- C It shows the horse has a scar on one side.
- D It shows the boy enjoys playing outdoors.

Objective 2

32 In the story, why does the young boy like to whistle?

- A He thinks the horse likes to hear people whistle.
- B He wants to show that he is acting like his father.
- C He believes that whistling makes him feel calm.
- D He thinks whistling excites the horse.

Objective 2

33 Which of these best describes the feelings of the boy in paragraph 9?

- A He is happy the horse likes him.
- B He is angry at Old Man Wiggins for trying to kill the horse.
- C He thinks the horse is really a champion race horse.
- D He is nervous about what the horse might do to him.

Objective 2

34 Why did the young boy leave carrots by the fence for the horse?

- A He was trying to get the horse to enter a fenced-in area.
- B The horse belonged to Old Man Wiggins.
- C He found the carrots and thought they belonged to the horse.
- D He was trying to become friends with the horse.

Objective 2

35 Read the chart below. It shows the order in which some events happened in the story.

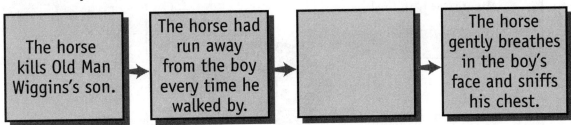

Which of these sentences belongs in the empty box?

A The horse calmly walks beside the young boy.
B The boy removes barbed wire from the horse's legs.
C The horse wiggles his ears as the boy walks by.
D The horse develops a scar on his side.

Objective 3

36 Read the first sentence in the summary below. Then answer the question that follows.

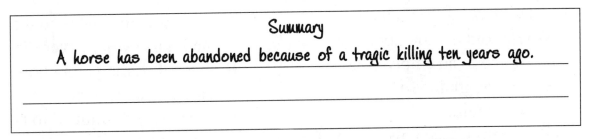

Which set of sentences best finishes the summary of the story?

A A young boy tries to make friends with the horse. The young boy whistles whenever he gets scared. He whistles when he is close to the horse.
B Old Man Wiggins tried to kill the horse and left a scar. Today, the horse sits unloved and uncared for in a field. A young boy feeds the horse carrots.
C A young boy feeds the horse carrots. Despite his fears he frees it from barbed wire that has become tangled around its feet. The boy and horse start to become friends.
D As a result the horse has been named "Killer" by its owner. A young boy calls the horse "Champ." He feeds it carrots and wistles to it.

Objective 1

37 Which of these words best completes a description of the horse?

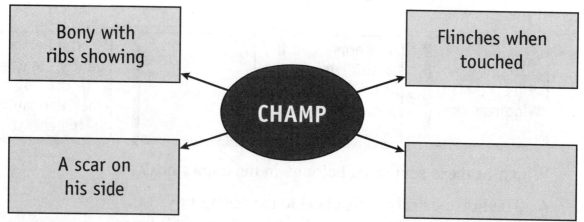

- **A** Unafraid
- **B** Well-fed
- **C** Mean and nasty
- **D** Mangy and fearful

Objective 3

38 What influence did the boy's father have on his son?

- **A** He taught his son how to deal with being frightened.
- **B** He told his son not to go home to an empty house.
- **C** He taught his son what to feed animals.
- **D** He introduced his son to Old Man Wiggins.

Objective 4

39 Which sentence from the story shows that the boy and the horse experienced similar feelings?

- **A** *The scar on his side was where Old Man Wiggins tried to kill him.*
- **B** *I could feel him trembling, and I thought he's as scared as I am.*
- **C** *When I was little and scared, Dad taught me to whistle.*
- **D** *Come on. I won't hurt you.*

Objective 4

40 If the story were continue, what would the next sentence in the story be likely to say?

- **A** That was the last time the boy and horse would ever met.
- **B** Each day, the young boy visited his new friend.
- **C** The horse continued to be frightened of the young boy.
- **D** The father insisted that the boy call the horse "Killer."

Objective 4

UNIT 4: THE WRITTEN COMPOSITION

In addition to the **TAKS Grade 4 in Reading,** you will be asked to take a writing test this year. The test will have two parts. In the first part, you will be asked to write a short composition. You will have some choice in what to write about. Your composition must respond to a **prompt** — something that encourages or "prompts" you to write. The prompt will be a short instruction, such as "Write a composition about a family trip." Your composition will then be scored based on five characteristics:

The second part of the test will examine your ability to revise and edit. You will be given a series of short passages of student writing. Each passage will be followed by multiple-choice questions asking you how to revise and correct sentences in the passage. For example, a question might ask:

> What change, if any, should be made in sentence 1?
> A Change *mispelling* to *misspelling*
> B Change *is* to *are*
> C Change *larger* to *largest*
> D Make no change

In this unit, you will learn ways to improve your writing skills — not only for the TAKS but for all your writing. You will learn about the five characteristics of good writing, the writing process, and the most important conventions of written English that fourth graders should know. You will also have many opportunities to practice your writing skills, so that you'll be able to perform your best when the day of the real test arrives.

CHAPTER 11

FOCUS AND COHERENCE

The writing prompt on the **TAKS Grade 4 in Writing** will be open-ended. An **open-ended prompt** does not tell you to write any particular kind of composition.

The choice of what type of composition you write — your purpose for writing — will be your own. However, you must write a *focused* and *coherent* composition that responds to the prompt. For example, the writing prompt on the **TAKS Grade 4 in Writing** might appear as follows:

Write a composition about a family trip.

The information in the box below will help you remember what you should think about when you write your composition.

REMEMBER — YOU SHOULD

- ❏ write about a family trip
- ❏ make sure that each sentence you write helps the reader understand your composition
- ❏ write about your ideas in detail so that the reader really understands what you are saying
- ❏ try to use correct spelling, capitalization, punctuation, grammar and sentences

DIFFERENT PURPOSES FOR WRITING

There are many ways that you could respond to the prompt on the previous page. For example, you could:

★ **Write to Inform.** You could write an essay informing readers about the different trips a family can take — to visit natural wonders like the Grand Canyon, to historic locations like the Alamo, or just to have fun at Disney World.

★ **Write to Influence.** You could write a persuasive essay arguing that Americans should take more family trips together.

★ **Write to Entertain.** You could write a short story about an imaginary family in the future that takes an exciting trip to the planet Mars.

★ **Write to Express.** You could write a personal narrative about a memorable trip you took with your family and why you enjoyed it.

FOCUS

When your eyes are focused on something, you see it clearly. Writing is *focused* when its object remains sharply in view. On the **TAKS Grade 4 in Writing,** the prompt will suggest a general range of topics you can write about.

An object in focus remains sharply in view.

In the prompt on the previous page, you could decide to write about any family trip. Even though the prompt is open-ended, remember you still must write about a family trip. Within that broad field, you must choose a more specific topic to write about. Think of the prompt as a launching pad for ideas. In the above examples of different purposes for writing, each suggested type of writing would provide a composition of some kind about family trips.

Once you have selected your specific topic and your purpose for writing (*such as to inform or entertain*), your writing should stay focused on the topic you have chosen.

Approach the writing prompt as a crossroads. Once you have decided which road to take, you must stay on that path until you complete your journey — a finished composition in response to the prompt.

YOUR TOPIC AS AN UMBRELLA

Think of your topic as an umbrella that covers your entire composition. Ideas and details that come under that imaginary umbrella are within the focus of your composition. Anything that falls outside this umbrella should be left out. Avoid including information that is *unrelated* to your topic. Information is unrelated when it does not tell the reader anything about the topic you are writing about:

★ If you decided to write a **personal narrative** about a memorable family trip, your composition should stay focused on this topic. Details about where your family went, what they saw, and how they got along would all be within the focus of your composition. However, writing about your parents' jobs or what you like to eat would be unrelated, unless these facts influenced your trip in some way.

★ If you chose to write an *informative essay* about different types of family trips, everything in your essay should directly relate to that theme. Information about seaside holidays would be within the focus of your essay. However, detailed information about the plants and animals found along  the Gulf of Mexico might not be related to the topic of your composition.

You can keep your composition focused and avoid including unrelated information by careful planning in the prewriting stage. When you later revise your essay, be sure to take out any unrelated information. Be sure to include enough information to give your composition a sense of **completeness.** Your reader should understand your main ideas and the details that support them. Your composition should be *focused* so the reader can easily see how your ideas relate to each other and to the topic as a whole.

FOCUSED PARAGRAPHS

A **paragraph** is a group of related sentences on a single topic. Just as your composition should be focused as a whole, each paragraph should also be focused.

In *informative* and *persuasive* writing, most paragraphs will have a **topic sentence** — a sentence that introduces the theme of the paragraph to the reader. The rest of the paragraph should stay focused on that topic. The paragraph of a *fictional story* or *personal narrative* may describe a place, person, or event without a topic sentence. Each paragraph should still stay focused on one distinct subject.

COHERENCE

Coherence refers to how well the parts of your composition stick together. Your paragraphs should be linked to one another and to your main topic to add to the coherence of your composition. The reader should be able to easily see how your ideas and details are connected to the topic and to one another. Staying focused on a single topic will help your composition stay coherent. The organization of your writing and the use of **transition words** will also strengthen its coherence. You will learn more about transition words in a later chapter.

FOCUS AND COHERENCE

DOs	DON'Ts
★ Do write about a topic connected to the prompt.	★ Don't write about something unrelated to the prompt.
★ Do maintain clear relationships between your ideas.	★ Don't include unrelated information outside the focus of your topic.
★ Do provide a sense of completeness.	★ Don't make sudden shifts from one idea to another without transitions.
★ Do include a meaningful introduction and conclusion.	
★ Do keep your composition focused on your main idea or theme.	

CHAPTER 12

THE DEVELOPMENT OF IDEAS

When you choose a specific topic to write about in response to the prompt, always try to pick something you really know and care about. This will make it easier for you to think of ideas and details to include. On the **TAKS Grade 4 in Writing,** how well you develop your ideas will affect your score.

DEVELOPING YOUR MAIN IDEA

You may have one idea or central message about your topic. You should also develop several supporting ideas. Use specific details to explain or illustrate each of these supporting ideas. These details could be facts to support a persuasive argument, descriptions to illustrate a story, or examples to prove a general point. On the TAKS, you can even make up some details to develop your ideas. A diagram of your composition might appear as follows:

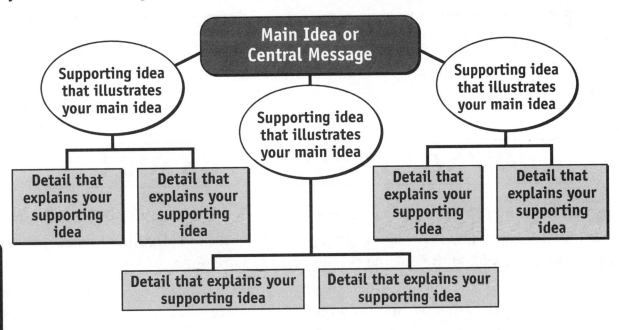

Think about the *who, what, when, where* and *how* for each detail you provide. Use all of your senses to describe places, people, and events in your composition. The reader should be able to picture in his or her own mind the same thoughts that you were expressing when you wrote. Details help your reader to make a clearer mental picture.

A good writer is able to write down thoughts in a way that the reader can picture the same thoughts. Clear and precise details help in this process.

Make sure your ideas and details clearly relate to the focus of your composition. When you edit and revise, cross out any ideas or details that do not support your main idea or theme.

HOW TO DEVELOP YOUR IDEAS

Including more supporting ideas and details can help you to raise the score your composition will receive. Developing your ideas more fully also makes you a better writer. Look at the outline on the following page, based on one student's composition. A close look at this outline can help you to see why the composition created from this outline only received a score of 2. As you can see from examining this outline, this student failed to fully develop his or her ideas. The composition lacked a depth of detail and support.

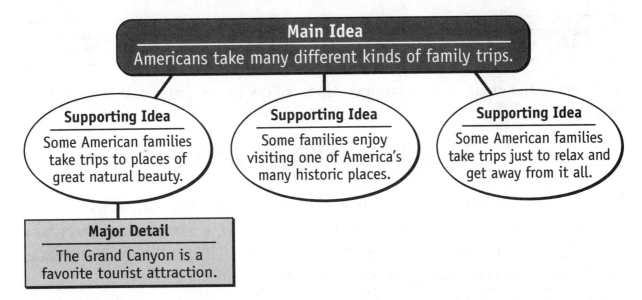

Compare this outline for a composition with the outline below. The composition using this outline received a higher score. Can you see why?

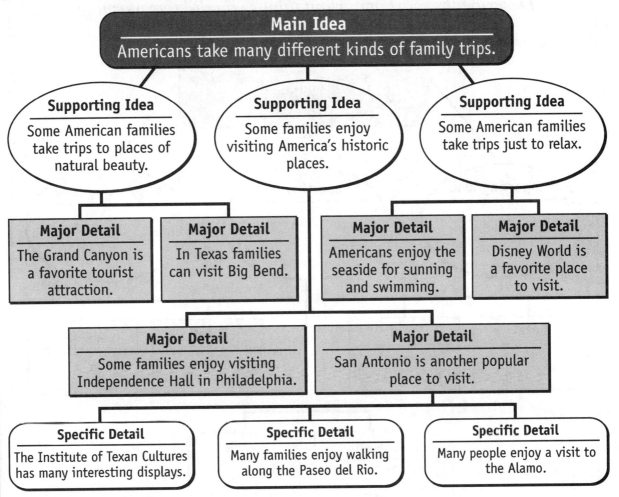

HINTS TO DEVELOP YOUR MAIN IDEA

To develop the ideas of your composition, follow these hints for different types of writing:

WHEN YOU NARRATE

If you are telling about an experience, develop your composition by describing each important event in detail. Tell about the *who, what, when, where, how,* and *why* of each event. Be as specific as you can. This will help your reader picture what you are writing about in your composition.

CHECKING YOUR UNDERSTANDING

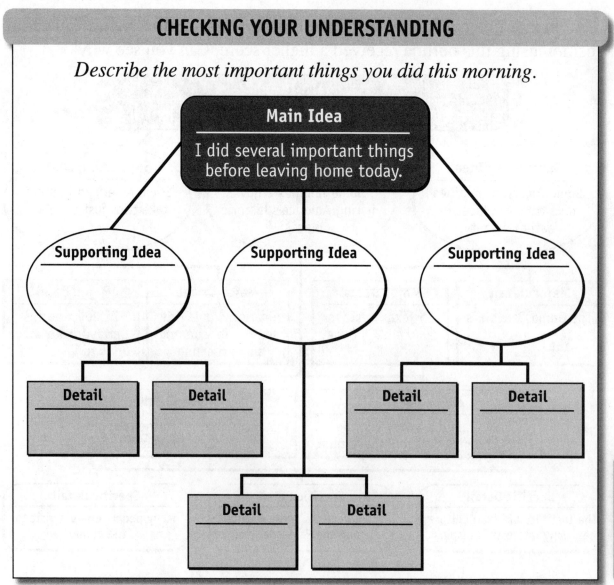

WHEN YOU WRITE TO INFORM

When writing to inform, develop your composition by providing specific ideas, facts, details, and examples to support each part of your explanation. Put yourself in the reader's shoes. Think about what your reader needs to know in order to understand what you are explaining.

CHECKING YOUR UNDERSTANDING

Provide details for an essay about a popular activity or pastime:

What is it? _____

When do people usually do it? _____

Where do people do it? _____

How do people do it? _____

Why do people do it? _____

WHEN YOU WRITE TO PERSUADE

When you take a position on an issue, develop your composition by giving reasons for adopting your position. For each reason, list or describe specific ideas, details, and examples that explain or support your position.

DO NOT BE AFRAID TO TAKE AN UNUSUAL APPROACH

Do not be afraid to approach your topic *from an unusual viewpoint,* to *reveal your true feelings,* or to *make interesting connections between ideas*. Fresh approaches like these make your writing more interesting. However, do not wait for the day of the TAKS to practice taking risks. Experiment with your classroom assignments and other writing so that you're comfortable taking risks when the test comes. For example:

★ Pretend you are a character with a unique point of view. You might relate a story or some other writing from the eyes of a witness or friend. For instance, you could tell a story about a family trip to Disney World from the standpoint of a worker in the park.

★ Write about an event that truly moved you. Connect with your innermost feelings and put them down on paper. Tell about a time you were very happy or sad. What was moving for you is likely to be moving for others.

★ Make up some facts to dress up your writing. Allow your thoughts and creativity to stretch your imagination. Write to express or entertain. Don't be afraid to create details to make your account more interesting.

Think about the ideas and details someone reading your composition would like to know. See how much more interesting and fun writing can be.

THE DEVELOPMENT OF IDEAS

DOs	DON'Ts
★ Do choose something to write about that you know well and have ideas about.	★ Don't write without first thinking about your ideas, how they are connected, and how you can illustrate or explain them.
★ Do present a number of ideas to support or explain your main idea or theme.	
★ Do develop each idea thoroughly with examples, sensory details, illustrative events, facts, and quotations.	★ Don't just list your ideas without explaining them.
	★ Don't make your ideas so vague that readers cannot understand them.
★ Do take risks in writing, such as writing from an unusual viewpoint.	★ Don't leave out important information, creating gaps between your ideas.

CHAPTER 13

ORGANIZATION

Organization refers to how you bring your ideas and details together. Imagine someone who built a house with the roof at the bottom and the basement on top. The house would surely soon collapse! In the same way, all your writing, including your response on the **TAKS Grade 4 in Writing,** has to be put together in a *logical* and *orderly* way. If your organization is  not logical, your reader will not be able to follow what you are writing about.

There are many ways to organize an essay or story. In most cases, your composition should be organized into three main parts: an *introduction, body,* and *conclusion.* Let's look at each of these parts more closely.

 ## THE INTRODUCTION

When we first meet someone, we introduce ourselves. Similarly, a composition should begin with an **introduction** that tells the reader what it is you are writing about. You can begin your introduction in many different ways. Try to think of a "grabber lead" that will really interest your readers. Do not be afraid to "spice up" your writing a little. For example, suppose you were asked to write a composition about families. Since you just studied bees in science you decide to write about how honeybees live together as a family in hives. On the following page are several interesting ways you might consider to open your composition:

Type of Opening	Example	Now You Try One on Any Subject:
State a Surprising Fact	A single queen bee can control hundreds of other bees in a hive.	
Propose a Question	Did you ever think about what an amazing family a beehive is?	
Create a Dialogue	"Don't move," I screamed at my brother. "You're surrounded by thousands of bees."	
Preview the Main Points	Scientist have identified three main reasons why honeybees are so successful. They work together; they adapt easily to different climates; and they lay large numbers of eggs.	
Provide a Quotation	"A honeybee hive is similar to a giant family," scientists tell us.	
Provide a Detailed Description	Mike climbed onto the roof of his car. As far as he could see, clouds of bees, forming one giant family, approached from all directions.	
Introduce the Setting, Narrator, or Main Characters	My adventure began in the woods of Yellowstone Park, one of America's most scenic and beautiful destinations. In front of me hung a large beehive.	

These are just some of the ways to begin a composition. The key is to think of a "grabber lead" that will interest readers and make them want to know more about what you are writing. Again, do not wait for the TAKS to try out these different openings. Use them in your classwork assignments and other writing.

THE BODY

The body is the main part of your composition. In the body, you must provide supporting ideas and details to explain your main idea or theme.

Be sure to present these ideas and details in some logical order. This makes it easy for the reader to follow your ideas. The way you organize your writing will depend on what you are writing about. Good writers use many ways to organize their ideas logically. You learned about most of these ways when you learned how readings are organized, earlier in this book.

★ **Time Order.** If you are telling about an event or experience, the first paragraph can provide an umbrella statement identifying the entire experience you are writing about. Then provide details about each event in the order in which it happened.

★ **Cause-and-Effect Order.** If you are explaining the *causes* and *effects* of an important event, one way is to begin by describing all of the causes. After you have described the causes of the event, then describe the event and its effects. Another way to write 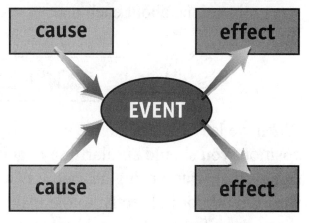 about causes and effects is to describe each cause and its particular effects, one at a time. This works well with a series of events.

★ **Space Order.** If you are describing an object or scene in your writing, imagine the object or scene in your mind. Then pick some point and begin to describe it. Move left to right, or up and down, as you continue your description. Be sure to continue in the same direction for the rest of the description.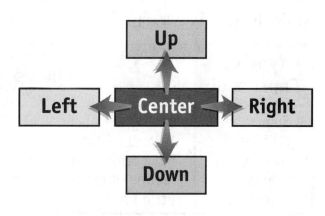

★ **Order of Importance.** If you have a main idea and several supporting details, give the main idea first. Then provide the supporting details in the order of their importance. You can give the most important detail first, or start with the least important detail and move to the most important. You can use the same pattern of organization in presenting points in a persuasive essay.

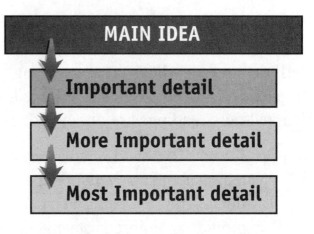

★ **Compare and Contrast.** To *compare* and *contrast* two or more things, first identify what you are comparing. Then it is often helpful to tell what they have in common. Finally, tell about their differences — what is unique about each one.

 # CONCLUSION

When we leave someone, we normally say good-bye. At the end of your composition, you should similarly say "good-bye" to your reader. The **conclusion** signals that your writing has come to an end. Usually the writer refers in some way, directly or indirectly, to the main idea or theme of the writing. There are many ways for you to conclude your composition. Suppose the prompt called for you to write a composition about a family trip. You decide to write about a trip your family took to San Antonio. On that trip, your little brother got lost while the family was strolling along the famous River Walk.

Type of Conclusion	Example	Now You Try One on Any Subject:
Summarize the main ideas of the body of your writing.	Seeing the Alamo and visiting the Texan Institute of Cultures was fun, but nothing could compare with the feeling of losing and then finding my little brother.	

Type of Conclusion	Example	Now You Try One on Any Subject:
State some general lesson that can be learned from what you have written.	The panic we shared when my little brother was lost taught us what being a family is all about. It is our responsibility to look out for each other's safety and protection.	
When writing a story, solve the conflict you created in the story.	We took family trips again, but nothing could ever compare with that memorable visit to San Antonio. When my little brother got lost, I thought my mother would die of fear. Even I was happy to find him. I guess I really do love him after all.	
End with a question of importance that your composition raised.	Sometimes my little brother seems annoying. I almost wish he wasn't there. Then I think of our trip to San Antonio. Do we really appreciate another person only when he is no longer around?	
State an opinion about the topic you wrote about.	Sometimes a trip can bring family members together. Sometimes a trip can tear them apart. In our case, it made us appreciate my brother.	
Finish with a quotation or saying.	There is a question raised in the Bible: "Am I my brother's keeper?" On this trip, I guess I learned that I was.	
Recommend or use a call to action.	To prevent mistakes like this from happening again, make sure you buddy up with your younger brother.	
Use a "circular ending" — end by returning to the beginning.	As we drove away from San Antonio, the skyline in the distance looked just as it did the day we arrived. But our feelings about each other had changed, even if the city was still the same.	

Again, do not wait until the day of the TAKS to practice with different types of conclusions. Practice using them in your daily writing.

MEANINGFUL TRANSITIONS

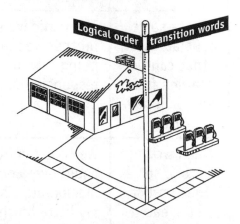

To make the organization of your ideas and supporting details clearer to the reader, you should use **transition words** and **transition phrases.** These words and phrases act as signposts. They tell the reader that you are moving from one point or event in your writing to another. When readers see these signposts, they know they are moving in another direction. Transitions serve to connect ideas and events that might otherwise seem unrelated. They help the reader move from one idea or event to another. Choose your transitions carefully to indicate the correct relationship between the sentences and paragraphs they connect.

TIME AND PLACE

Some transition words and phrases show there has been a change in *time* or *place:*

> He ate dinner at 7 o'clock. *Later that evening,* he went to bed.

Changes in Time and Place

after	the next day	then
before	the following week	next
finally	later	meanwhile

While and *meanwhile* are special types of transitions. They usually indicate a change of place during the same time:

> Tom was working in Houston.
> *Meanwhile,* Cheryl was eating lunch in Dallas.

NEW POINTS OR EXAMPLES

Transitions can be used when you are moving from one argument to the next:

> *A second reason* for inspecting luggage at all airports more carefully is to keep people from taking weapons on airplanes.

Here are some other transition words and phrases for listing points in an argument or introducing specific examples:

Listing Points in an Argument	
first	the most important reason
second	in addition
Introducing Examples	
for example	indeed
in fact	in particular

INTRODUCING DIFFERENCES

Transitions sometimes introduce something that is different to what has already been said. For example, the word *however* marks a contrast or changes the direction of the argument:

> Usually I enjoy jogging. *However,* in the summer heat I prefer to go swimming.

Below are several transition words and phrases for introducing a contrast:

Introducing Differences		
however	but	despite
nevertheless	yet	on the other hand
even so	even though	in spite of this

CONCLUSIONS

Transitions can also be used to indicate a conclusion or the end of an argument:

> *Therefore,* he had no choice but to help his teacher.

Here are some transition words and phrases for introducing a conclusion, cause or effect:

Introducing Conclusions, Causes or Effects		
as a result	due to	in conclusion
in consequence	for this reason	thus
because of	therefore	since

ORGANIZATION

DOs	DON'Ts
★ Do create a plan for presenting your ideas.	★ Don't present ideas in a random, haphazard way.
★ Do present ideas in a logical order that will be clear to your reader.	★ Don't repeat ideas unnecessarily, preventing the development of ideas.
★ Do connect paragraphs and sentences with meaningful transitions.	★ Don't use a lot of words to say nothing.
★ Do use different types of transitions.	★ Don't write without using transitions.

CHAPTER 14

VOICE

Not everyone wears the same style of jeans. People wear different styles to express themselves. Just as with clothing, there are different styles in writing. **Voice** refers to how your writing expresses your personal style. Does your writing sound authentic and honest to the reader? Does it express your unique individuality and point of view? Or does your writing seem stuffy and fake? An authentic voice will connect with and interest the reader. Be true to yourself!

You can show your originality and creativity by the way in which you decide to present your essay or story. To develop a distinctive voice, think about your readers and the impression you want to make on them. The impression you make will depend on the *type of writing*, its *tone*, your *choice of words*, and *sentence patterns*.

TONE

The **tone** of your writing shows your feelings towards what you are writing about. Your tone may be witty, sarcastic, critical, funny, sad, or enthusiastic. Make sure your tone fits the content and purpose of your composition. For example, humor would not seem right if you were writing a science report or describing a tragic event. Keep your tone in tune with the subject:

★ If you are writing an **informative essay,** the tone is usually neutral and formal. See if you can write about your subject without using "I" as the narrator. Readers should feel your essay is accurately telling the facts.

★ If you are writing a **narrative story,** you might tell the story through the eyes of one of the characters. You can write in the "first person," using "I." The style and tone should be more personal and informal.

★ If you are writing a **persuasive essay,** introduce your main points and explain each of them in a logical but forceful manner.

Your approach to the topic and your tone should always be appropriate to what you are trying to achieve in your writing.

WORD CHOICE

A very important part of *voice* is your **choice of words.** Interesting words get the reader involved in your composition. They are specific and descriptive. They help the reader to form a mental picture of what you are writing about.

When writing, choose the most precise and descriptive words that you can. Avoid vague language. Words that help readers to *see, hear, taste, smell,* or *feel* what you are writing about make it easier for them to connect with your thoughts. It also makes your writing more interesting. For example, "shattered" is a more precise word than "broken" because it tells readers that something has broken into many tiny pieces — far too many to ever be repaired.

CHECKING YOUR UNDERSTANDING

For each pair of words check (✔) the word that is more precise.

- ☐ minivan *or* ☐ car
- ☐ galloped *or* ☐ went
- ☐ animal *or* ☐ dolphin
- ☐ vegetable *or* ☐ carrots
- ☐ ate *or* ☐ feasted
- ☐ store *or* ☐ mall

Add details to the words below so that the reader can see, hear, feel, or taste the word. For example, apple: a crisp, red apple with a tart taste.

table: _____   bike: _____

dress: _____   room: _____

IMAGERY

Imagery is a helpful tool you can use to liven up your writing. **Imagery** refers to word pictures used by writers to express feelings and ideas. For example, an author might want to express the idea that whispers are soft and gentle. To do this, the author might compare a *whisper* with *soft skin* — "She spoke in a whisper *as soft as skin*." In this sentence, you can almost sense the softness of her whisper. This is an example of one of the two most common forms of imagery — *similes* and *metaphors*. Each is a form of comparison:

★ A **simile** uses *like* or *as* to compare one thing to another.

- Her eyes sparkled *like* diamonds.
- The warrior fought *like* a tiger.

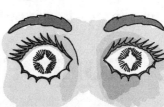

> Here a warrior is displaying the characteristics of a tiger — the warrior fought with the viciousness of a tiger.

★ A **metaphor** compares two things without using *like* or *as*. You simply describe something as something else:

- She was an *angel*.
- He had a *heart of gold*.

> Here we can imagine two people so nice that one is like an angel and the other's kindness is as valuable as gold.

CHECKING YOUR UNDERSTANDING

1. Use a *simile* in a sentence about your classroom. _____

2. Use a *metaphor* in a sentence about your school. _____

You will not be allowed to write poetry or "rap" for your TAKS composition. However, like a fine poet or a good rapper, you should think about your choice of words and use imagery to create your own distinctive style and voice.

SENTENCE PATTERNS

Just as good writers consider their choice of words carefully, they also think about and vary their sentence patterns. This makes their writing more interesting to the reader. If all your sentences were of the same length and same style, your composition would be dull instead of interesting to read.

COMPOUND SUBJECTS AND VERBS

Some sentences have two subjects with one verb, or one subject with two verbs:

> *Jack* and *Jill* **went up the hill.**
> **Jack** *fetched* **a pail of water and** *slid* **down the hill.**

COMPOUND SENTENCES

A **compound sentence** joins together two *independent sentences* with a conjunction — **and, or, but, yet.** Always put a comma before this kind of conjunction when you make a compound sentence.

> *Jack went up the hill,* **and** *Jill went to fetch a pail of water.*
> *Jack liked soda,* **but** *Jill preferred to drink tea.*

COMPLEX SENTENCES

A *clause* has a subject and predicate, but it may not be a complete sentence. A complex sentence is made up of a main clause and one or more dependent clauses. Dependent clauses are introduced by words like **because, since, as, while,** or **who.**

> ***Jack could not climb the hill*** because *he was tired.*
> ***Jack,*** who *was tired,* ***could not climb the hill.***

The main clause (*Jack could not climb the hill*) is a sentence on its own, but the dependent clause (*because he was tired*) is not. It is introduced by a subordinate conjunction (***although, since, when, because, for, while***) or, in the second example, a relative pronoun (***who, which, that***).

VOICE

DOs	DON'Ts
★ Do write about something that really interests you.	★ Don't write in a way that is stiff and artificial.
★ Do express your individuality and unique viewpoint.	★ Don't be afraid to be original or to express your own personal style.
★ Do think about your audience and purpose for writing.	★ Don't follow a formula in writing.
★ Do make expressive word choices and use imagery and different types of sentence patterns.	★ Don't use words that are not part of standard written English.

WRITING CONVENTIONS

Over the years, certain rules have developed for good writing. These cover ***sentence construction*** — avoiding sentence fragments and run-on sentences; ***usage*** — choosing the correct word based on the subject-verb agreement, pronoun forms, and other rules; and ***mechanics*** — spelling, capitalization, and punctuation. These rules are often known as "writing conventions." You will review these when you study for the ***revising and editing*** part of the test.

Chapter 15

THE WRITING PROCESS

It is difficult to create a polished piece of writing all at once. Writers have to go through a **process** — developing, writing, and revising their ideas. There are five main steps in the writing process. These steps apply to responding to the writing prompt on the TAKS as well as to all your other writing:

THE WRITING PROMPT

The writing prompt on the **TAKS Grade 4 in Writing** will actually have several parts:

★ **The Writing Task.** The first part of the writing prompt will give you a writing task.

★ **A Reminder Checklist.** The second part of the writing prompt will have a list of reminders for you to think about as you write.

★ **The Writing Pages.** Your answer sheet will have several lined pages for you to write your final draft. Your question booklet will have space for you to plan your composition and write a first draft.

You will have as long as you need to complete your work. The **TAKS Grade 4 in Writing** is not a timed test.

Let's begin by looking at a sample writing prompt:

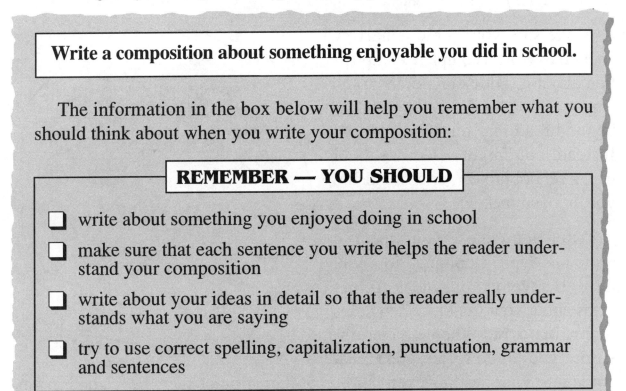

STEP 1: PLAN AND PREWRITE

The first step in the writing process is to plan what you will write. For many students, this is the hardest part of responding to a writing prompt. You need to think of what you want to write about and what type of composition you wish to complete.

In deciding what to write about, use your own knowledge and experiences. Think about what you have personally experienced, read about, or learned from others that relates to the prompt. In this case, you should begin by jotting down a list of interesting things you have done in school.

Review your list and pick the best one to write about. Next, think about what kind of composition you want to write. For example, you might choose a *persuasive essay,* a *narrative* based on your personal experiences, a *make-believe story,* or an *informative essay.*

Make sure your topic is narrow enough to write a complete composition about it. For example, the topic "my year at school" would probably be too broad for your composition. Instead, you might select a school trip, a school project, or a friendship you enjoyed making.

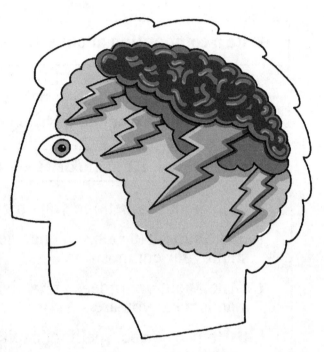

After you choose your specific topic and type of composition, you need to develop your ideas. To get ideas about your topic, it often helps to **brainstorm.** When you brainstorm, you jot down any ideas that come into your head — even if some of them do not seem very good. Afterwards, you review the list you made to see which ideas are really good enough to use. Some people prefer to jot down their thoughts without a plan to see where those thoughts take them. This would be a good approach for a journal, but it is not suggested for this test. You need to use some kind of plan to ensure that your writing stays on track!

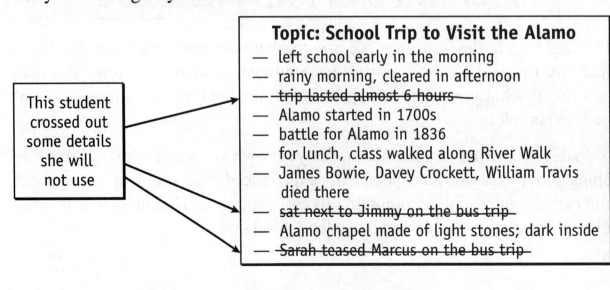

This student crossed out some details she will not use

Topic: School Trip to Visit the Alamo
— left school early in the morning
— rainy morning, cleared in afternoon
— ~~trip lasted almost 6 hours~~
— Alamo started in 1700s
— battle for Alamo in 1836
— for lunch, class walked along River Walk
— James Bowie, Davey Crockett, William Travis died there
— ~~sat next to Jimmy on the bus trip~~
— Alamo chapel made of light stones; dark inside
— ~~Sarah teased Marcus on the bus trip~~

Whatever type of composition you choose to write, you should next organize your points through some form of prewriting plan. Use the page where the prompt appears in your test booklet as a convenient place to plan your response.

Think carefully as you plan. If you cannot clearly picture what you are trying to say in your own mind, you will not be able to communicate it clearly to others to understand. Since each person is unique, there is no single magic formula for planning a composition that works best for everyone. There are several ways you might consider for prewriting your response.

CLUSTER OR WEB

One prewriting format is **clustering** or **webbing.** To create a cluster or web, put your topic or controlling idea in the middle of the paper. Branch out or surround this idea or topic with supporting facts, details, and examples. Then surround these details with further descriptive information. Here is what a prewriting cluster might look like for an essay about a class trip to the Alamo:

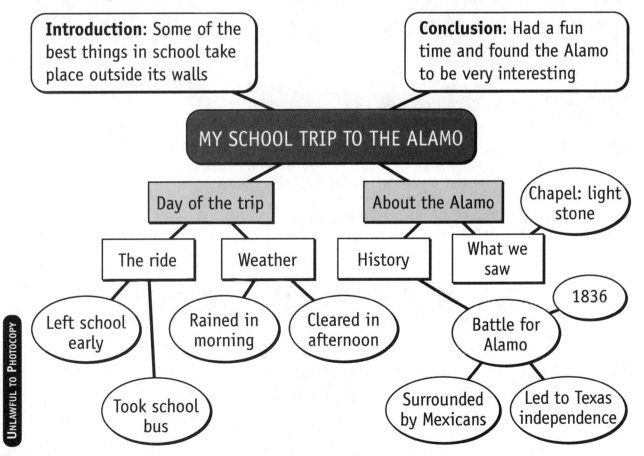

OUTLINE

An outline is used by writers to help break down large ideas, events, or concepts into smaller units. Writers generally use Roman (I, II, III) and Arabic numerals (1, 2, 3) as well as capital (A, B, C) and lower case letters (a, b, c) to make an outline. Here is what an outline for a school trip to the Alamo might look like:

MY CLASS TRIP TO THE ALAMO

I. **Introduction:** Some of the best things in school take place outside its walls.

II. **Body:**
    A. The Bus Ride
        1. Left school early
        2. Took school bus to get there

    B. Weather
        1. Rained in the morning
        2. Cleared up in the afternoon

    C. Lunch along the River Walk

    D. The Alamo
        1. History
            a. Started in the 1700s
            b. Battle for Alamo: 1836, Bowie, Crockett, Travis killed
        2. What we saw
            a. Alamo chapel: light stone, dark inside

III. **Conclusion:** Why the trip was fun and interesting

THE HAMBURGER OUTLINE

Another prewriting method is to outline your answer in the form of a hamburger. This form is especially useful for writing informative essays and reports. There are three main parts to a hamburger outline:

The **top bun** is the place where you identify your main idea or the position you are taking in response to the prompt.

The **patties of meat** make up the body of your paper. Here is where you list reasons, specific details and examples to support the main idea. Think of these details as the lettuce, tomatoes, and ketchup that give flavor to your writing. Use more than one patty to represent different paragraphs.

The **bottom bun** is where you summarize your main ideas or remind the reader of your strongest points.

After you complete your prewriting plan, review it carefully:

- ☐ Does your plan respond to the prompt?
- ☐ Have you left out any important information?
- ☐ Is there any unimportant or unrelated information you should take out?
- ☐ Should some points be moved around to improve the organization?

Remember, it is much easier to change the organization of your essay in the planning stage than after you have written a complete draft.

STEP 2: DRAFT YOUR COMPOSITION

Next in the writing process, you turn your outline, cluster, hamburger outline or other prewriting plan into a **first draft.** Turn each point of your plan into one or more complete sentences. Remember to organize your writing into three parts — an *introduction, body,* and *conclusion.* Also make sure the body of your essay is logically organized and stays focused on your topic and main idea.

You can write the body of your paper first and then write the introduction after you see what you have written for the main part of your composition. Do not worry too much about organization or grammatical errors. Your main focus at this early stage is to get your ideas down on paper. Additional ideas and details should come to mind as you write.

Remember, you are trying to get your reader to "see" what is in your imagination. One of the best ways to do this is to be as descriptive as possible. A simple way to accomplish this is to use all five of your **senses** in describing things.

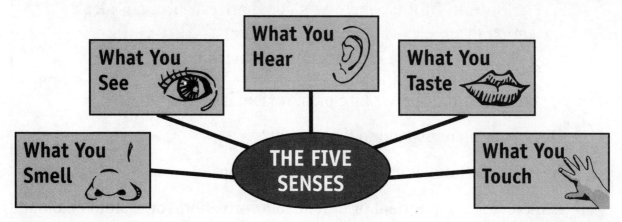

STEP 3: REVISE YOUR COMPOSITION

During the third step of the writing process, you should reread your first draft and reorganize and correct it. During the revision process, you should focus on ideas, organization, and voice rather than on writing conventions. Read your draft silently to yourself. Pretend you are someone else, reading the draft for the very first time. Make sure you have included all of your major ideas. Check that the ideas and details in your writing relate to your topic and main idea.

Pay close attention to the organization of your draft. Ask yourself if your ideas and supporting details are presented in the best order. Even after your draft is completed, you can move sentences or whole paragraphs around simply by using arrows to show where they should go.

As you review your composition, ask yourself the following questions:

REVISING CHECKLIST

1. **Do I need to add any information?**
   - ❏ Do I have a good introduction and conclusion?
   - ❏ Have I included all the important details, examples, or facts?
   - ❏ Have I used my five senses?

2. **Do I need to remove any information?**
   - ❏ Have I stuck to my topic?
   - ❏ Have I repeated myself where I didn't need to?
   - ❏ Have I included details not related to the main idea?

3. **Do I need to rewrite any parts?**
   - ❏ Are there any ideas or sentences that are unclear?

4. **Do I need to move any parts?**
   - ❏ Are my sentences in the best order?
   - ❏ Do any ideas or details seem out of place?

STEP 4: EDITING

After you revise your composition, you will need to **edit** your work for errors in writing conventions. You will learn more about these conventions in later chapters. The checklist that follows can help you to edit your paper:

EDITING CHECKLIST

Sentence Structure
- ☐ Does every sentence have a subject and predicate (*verb*)?
- ☐ Did I write any sentence fragments or run-on sentences?
- ☐ Did I vary my sentence patterns?

Capitalization
- ☐ Did I start each sentence with a capital letter?
- ☐ Are all proper nouns (*particular people and things*) capitalized?

Word Choice / Usage
- ☐ Does my composition express my unique personal style?
- ☐ Did I use precise, descriptive words (*fluffy, wrinkled, bitter*)?
- ☐ Do all the subjects and verbs agree?

Punctuation
- ☐ Did I use the correct punctuation to end each sentence?
- ☐ Did I use commas before coordinate conjunctions (*and, but, or*)?
- ☐ Did I correctly use quotation marks to report direct speech?

Spelling
- ☐ Have I spelled every word correctly?

STEP 5: WRITE YOUR FINAL DRAFT

After revising and editing your first draft, you are ready to write your final draft. Copy your work neatly onto the lined paper in the response booklet. Be sure to make all the corrections and changes you added to your first draft as you copy your text. Pay attention to the presentation of your work. Keep a margin on both sides of the paper. Begin each paragraph on a new line. Indent each new paragraph. Give your final draft a neat appearance that is easy to read. Write and erase neatly. Even if you write your final draft carefully, you may still make mistakes. After you complete your final draft, read your work over one last time. Look for any new errors. Write any additions above the line with a "caret" mark (∧) to show where they go.

CHAPTER 16

WRITING FOR DIFFERENT PURPOSES

As you know, you will have a choice of what to write about on the **TAKS**. Based on the prompt, you will have to choose a specific topic and type of writing. Three of the most common types of writing are a *personal narrative, imaginary story,* and *informative essay.*

Each of these writing types has its own method of organization, purpose, and tone. You may mix and combine several of these types in writing your composition. For example, an imaginary short story may have some paragraphs that are informative. However, a writer often sticks to one type of writing and you should know the main features of each type.

WRITING TO EXPRESS

In a **personal narrative,** the writer gives an account of something that has happened to him or her. Often the purpose of the writer is to express his or her feelings about a topic. On the **TAKS Grade 4,** you may choose to write about an experience that actually happened to you.

Show, don't tell. This means you should be sure to provide plenty of details to *show* what is happening. The reader should have the feeling of witnessing actual events. Let's begin exploring personal narratives by looking at a sample writing prompt:

> **Write a composition about an interesting person.**

There are many approaches you could take to respond to this prompt. For example, you could write an informative essay describing a famous person you have studied. Let's suppose you decided to write a personal narrative about someone you actually know. Your first task is to choose an interesting person to write about. The simplest way to begin is by thinking about all the interesting people you know. Make a list of the most interesting possibilities. Brainstorm to think of as many interesting people as you can. Then choose one to write about.

Some interesting people I know:

1.

2.

3.

4.

The interesting person I want to write about is:
_____

Now write a sentence that tells what is most interesting about this person:
_____

This sentence can serve as the main idea or theme of your narrative. Next, you have to think of supporting ideas and details to explain and illustrate your main idea. Fill in the web that follows to recall details and to organize your thoughts. You could also use an outline or any other prewriting technique to plan your composition.

| How do you know this person? _____ | What is this person like? _____ |

Name of the Person: _____
Why this person is interesting: _____

| What has this person done that is interesting? _____ | What qualities helped make this person interesting? _____ |

You can use the information you have jotted down in your web to write the body of your narrative. Once you have completed your prewriting plan, you are ready to start your first draft. Be sure your narrative has a clear introduction, body, and conclusion. Let's briefly review each of these parts:

INTRODUCTION
★ The introduction provides the focus of your narrative. In this example, the introduction should identify the interesting person you selected. Begin with a "grabber lead" — an interesting fact or a stimulating question.

BODY
★ A narrative is usually organized in time order. To help you organize your writing, it may help to take your web, such as the one above, and number the points in the order in which you introduce them. Here you should write about some of the interesting things the person has done.

CONCLUSION
★ You can often refer to your opening statement in your conclusion. You may want to end with a famous saying, a moral, or an interesting question you want your readers to think about.

In a personal narrative, you will usually be telling about things you experienced directly. The tone you use is often very informal and personal — told from your own viewpoint, using "I" or "we." However, you could also write a narrative as an impartial narrator telling the story in the "**third person**:"

First-Person Writing	Third-Person Writing
I woke up at ten o'clock that night.	Tom woke up at ten o'clock that night.
Write a sentence in the "first person." _____	
Write a sentence in the "third person." _____	

When you write your narrative, use vivid words that appeal to as many of the five senses as you can. Use precise and descriptive words that provide plenty of information. This will help readers recreate your experiences.

A MODEL NARRATIVE

Look at the model web plan below for a personal narrative about an interesting person.

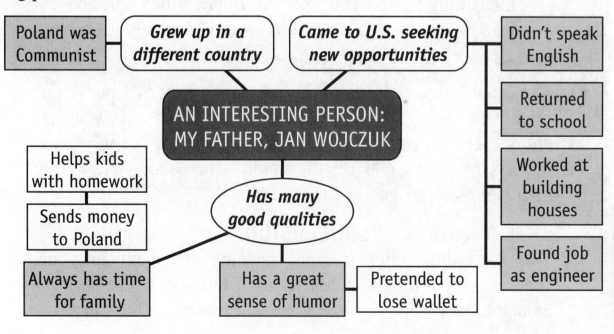

Here is a draft of the composition a student developed from the plan on the previous page in response to the prompt about an interesting person.

My Father, Jan Wojczuk: The Most Interesting Person I Know

Some people believe only rock singers, Hollywood stars, and famous people are interesting. I don't agree with them. Very often, the most interesting people are right under our own noses. I think the most interesting person I know is my own father, Jan Wojczuk.

My father did not grow up in the United States. He was born in a country in Europe called Poland. When he was growing up in Poland, the government was controlled by Communists. The government told people what to do most of the time. Opportunities were limited. One day, a cousin invited my father to the United States. My father did not speak English, and he was afraid to go, but he thought about the opportunities that existed in America. Then he finally changed his mind.

In the United States, he found work building houses. He worked very hard at his job. My father wanted more for his family, so he went back to school on weekends. First, he had to learn to speak English. Then, he began studying to become an engineer in the United States. Finally, he passed his test. Later, he started his own business.

His good qualities have helped him throughout his life. He has a great sense of humor. Once, he pretended to lose his wallet in the restaurant. My mother looked so nervous, until he told her it was only a joke. Then my father laughed so hard he fell off his seat right there in the restaurant. Everyone laughed. Even though he is always busy, he makes time for his family. He helps us with our homework and sends money to our grandparents, who still live in Poland.

It is great to be famous, but what really makes our nation great are people like my father. You probably never heard the name Jan Wojczuk. However, his kindness, hard work, and sense of humor make him the most interesting person I know!

Notice how this student author has added more details and fuller descriptions to the points found in her original plan. Each major point has become a separate paragraph of the composition.

WRITING TO ENTERTAIN

On the **TAKS Grade 4 in Writing,** you might also choose to make up your own fictional story based on the writing prompt. For example, you might write an imaginary short story about an interesting person. In writing your own original story, you will need to create:

Although there are many ways to create an original story, one of the best is to start by focusing on these elements — ***setting, characters,*** and ***plot.*** Plan your story around the topic suggested by the writing prompt. The plot should center on some problem the main characters have to resolve. Tell about events that happen to your characters as they try to resolve their problem. End your story by showing how the problem is resolved. Your conclusion might include a statement of your general theme or message.

You also need a narrator — someone who will tell the story. Your story can be told in the "third person" or by one of the characters. If you were asked to write a composition about an interesting person, your narrator would tell a story that shows just why the character is so interesting.

As always, you should begin your writing with some kind of plan. Jot down your ideas in note form or in some other prewriting format. For example, you could use the format of the "story board" on the next page to plan your story. Make your story about something that happens to an imaginary, but interesting person. You could make up a sorcerer, similar to the character of Harry Potter, or you could make up an imaginary "famous" person, like a rock star or athlete.

On the next page is a plan for a story about an interesting person living in England many years ago.

STORY BOARD

Setting: "Merry Old England"

Characters:
- ★ **Craig**, a master magician
- ★ **Alan**, the son of Craig, the magician
- ★ **King John**, the wicked ruler of Merry Old England

Plot:

★ *Main Conflict.* The King wants to know how Craig does his magic tricks. The evil king has Alan thrown into the castle dungeon. Craig wants to free his son from prison.

★ *Key Events.* Craig refuses to give away his magic secrets. Instead, he casts a spell on the people living in the castle. They cannot sleep.

★ King John refuses to free Alan from the dungeon. After some time, the king grows weary of not sleeping.

★ *Resolution.* When King John tires from not sleeping, he frees Alan. With his magic, Craig turns the king into a frog. Alan becomes the new king.

Theme: Part of what makes someone interesting is their fight against evil.

Now look at how the student author has started turning his plan into a first draft.

Once upon a time in Old England, there lived a magician named Craig. Craig was one of the most interesting people who ever lived. With his magic powers, he could move objects, make himself disappear, or cut people in half without hurting them.

In those days, England was ruled by King John, a wicked and evil king who was hated by his subjects. The king wanted to know Craig's secrets in performing magic so that he could make himself the world's most powerful ruler.

> King John offered riches to Craig, but the master magician refused to share a single secret with the wicked king. Finally, in anger, the king had his guards seize Craig's son, Alan. They threw him into the dungeon. "That will teach you to disobey your king!" the king shouted at Craig.
>
> From that moment, Craig could only think about how to free his son from the dungeon...

Now you should try to write a make-believe story of your own about an interesting person. Remember, in creative writing you can make up any characters, settings, or events that come to mind. Have fun writing a short story that you think will interest your reader. Use the story board below to develop your ideas.

STORY BOARD

Setting: _____

Characters:
- ★ _____
- ★ _____
- ★ _____

Plot:
- ★ *Main Conflict.* _____
- ★ *Key Events.* _____
- ★ *Resolution.* _____

Theme: _____

Now write a first draft of your story on a separate sheet of paper. Revise and edit your story and share it with your teacher and classmates. Make sure that it tells about an interesting person and has a conflict or problem that this character must resolve. Include details about the setting and other characters.

WRITING TO INFORM

On the **TAKS Grade 4 in Writing,** you might choose to write an **informative essay** in response to the prompt. Informative essays are one of the most common forms of writing. This kind of writing is used to *inform* readers — to give them information about something. People use informative writing to communicate messages, instructions, and ideas.

There are several types of informative writing. For example, you might *describe something, tell how two or more things are different or alike, explain why or how something happened,* or *tell why something is important.*

Let's look at what you could do for each of these types of essays:

★ To *describe* something, tell about its qualities. For example, to *describe* a favorite place, first identify that place. Then tell about its climate, how it looks, and what you can do there.

★ To *explain why or how* something happened, identify the causes that made it happen. Describe each cause and show how it helped lead to the event.

★ To *explain how* someone made a decision:
   (1) *identify* the problem the person faced;
   (2) *list the choices* the person had; and
   (3) *describe the steps* the person went through in making the decision.

★ To *explain why* something is *important,* you need to:
   (1) **describe** the item (*such as an invention or event*) and then
   (2) **tell about its immediate and long-term effects.** These effects are usually what makes it important. Think about how things were before the invention or event you have selected. Then think how things have changed as a result of the invention or event.

An informative essay is usually written in the third person. You should write as a neutral narrator without referring to yourself. This makes your writing seem more impartial and accurate.

You should begin your informative essay by thinking about what you want to write about. On a test like the TAKS, it may help to think about what you have recently studied in school. This may give you ideas for an informative essay. Make a list of possible topics to write about and choose the one you know the most about. For example, you may have studied Sam Houston in your social studies class. You might decide to use Sam Houston as the subject of your composition about an interesting person.

List of Famous People I Know Something About:

1. Sam Houston
2. The Tejana singer, Selena
3. The Civil Rights leader, Martin Luther King, Jr.
4.
5.

After you choose one of the topics from your list, brainstorm for ideas. Here you jot down everything you can remember about the person you have selected. Think about the **who, what, when, where, how,** and **why** of the person. For example:

- ★ When and where did the person live?
- ★ What was the person's background and education?
- ★ What did the person achieve?
- ★ What is it about the person that makes him or her so interesting?

Now you choose an interesting famous person to write about. First, complete the graphic organizer below.

TOPIC: _____

Supporting Facts and Details

Where and When: _____

Background and Education: _____

Personal Qualities: _____

Achievements: _____

What makes this person interesting: _____

Now write the first draft of your composition on a separate sheet of paper. Revise and edit your composition and share it with your classmates.

UNIT 5: PEER EDITING

The second part of the **TAKS Grade 4 in Writing** will examine your ability to revise and edit. You will be given a number of passages similar to those written by other fourth-grade students. These passages will have errors in their organization, sentence structures, usage and mechanics.

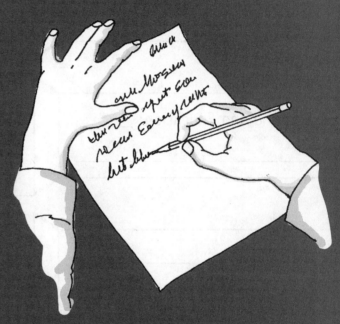

Your task on this part of the writing test will be to correct those errors. Each sentence in the passage will be numbered. Each passage will be followed by a number of multiple-choice questions, giving you an opportunity to add, revise or delete sentences.

This unit has three chapters:

★ **Chapter 17** examines paragraph organization and sentence construction. This chapter teaches you how to decide when to add or eliminate sentences. It will also show you how to recognize and correct sentence fragments and run-on sentences.

★ **Chapter 18** reviews the major rules of usage governing different parts of speech.

★ **Chapter 19** looks at mechanics — the rules governing punctuation, capitalization, and spelling.

Chapter 17

ORGANIZATION AND SENTENCE CONSTRUCTION

Some questions on the **TAKS Grade 4 in Writing** will ask you about the organization of a student passage and whether the sentences in the passage are correctly formed.

ORGANIZATION

To test your ability to improve the organization of a passage, the **TAKS Grade 4 in Writing** will ask you to add new sentences to a paragraph or take some sentences out. Remember that a *paragraph* is a group of related sentences that deal with the same topic. Often, the topic of the paragraph is stated near the beginning of the paragraph in a *topic sentence.* This topic sentence tells the main idea of the paragraph. Other sentences in the paragraph give further information about that main idea. Some paragraphs may not have a topic sentence. However, every paragraph will have a common theme even when there is no topic sentence directly stating it.

SENTENCES THAT DO NOT BELONG

On the TAKS, some sentences may not belong in the paragraph. These sentences will often be on the same topic as the composition as whole, but they will not be about the same aspect of the topic as the rest of the paragraph. In other words, the sentence does not belong in the paragraph because it does not relate to the other sentences in the paragraph. It does not explain, describe, or illustrate any of the other ideas in the paragraph. For example, which sentence does not belong in the paragraph on the next page?

> (1) The ancient Greeks believed that the actions of their gods and goddesses directly influenced what happened to ordinary people. (2) For example, a dispute among three goddesses supposedly led to the Trojan War. (3) Helen was the most beautiful woman in ancient Greece.

Which sentence does not belong? _____

Explain why you selected that sentence: _____

_____

ADDING SENTENCES

A good paragraph should be *complete*. It should explain its main idea clearly through examples, facts, and other supporting details. If a paragraph is incomplete, readers feel they need to know more to understand it.

Some questions on the **TAKS Grade 4 in Writing** will ask if a suggested sentence should be added to a paragraph. To answer this kind of question, first read the paragraph carefully. Then determine the topic of the paragraph. See which of the answer choices best relates to this same topic. If this sentence was added to the paragraph, would the paragraph be more complete and make better sense? Here is a sample question asking you whether to add a sentence to the paragraph at the top of this page:

1 Which sentence could **BEST** be added after sentence 2?

  A According to Greek legend, this war led to bloodshed and destruction among humans.
  B Roman religious beliefs were based on Greek ideas.
  C Helen loved a Trojan prince more than she loved her own husband.
  D The ancient Greeks did not face the same distractions we have today.

Here, the correct answer is **A.** This sentence further develops the theme of the paragraph that the actions of the gods influenced ordinary lives. It also adds important details showing how the Trojan War illustrates this.

STEPS FOR DECIDING WHEN TO DELETE OR ADD SENTENCES

(1) When you read a paragraph, first determine its topic.

(2) Look over each sentence as you read the paragraph. Ask yourself:
  ★ Does this sentence support the main topic of the paragraph?

(3) You may want to mark sentences that do not seem to belong by either <u>circling</u> or <u>underlining</u> them.

(4) Ask yourself whether the paragraph is complete.
  ★ Do all the supporting sentences sufficiently explain the main idea of the paragraph?
  ★ If the paragraph is not complete, what else is needed?

(5) Read over the answer choices carefully to see which sentence should be added or does not belong.

SENTENCE CONSTRUCTION

Another type of question on the revising and editing section of the TAKS will test your knowledge of **sentence structures.** These questions will ask you to correct a sentence fragment or a run-on sentence, or to combine or revise sentences.

SENTENCE FRAGMENTS

A **sentence fragment** is written with capitalization and punctuation as if it were a complete sentence, but it is not. A fragment either lacks a complete subject or verb, or it does not express a complete thought. When you read a sentence fragment, you have the feeling that something more should be coming.

> ★ **Lacks a Complete Thought.** Here are two examples of sentence fragments:
>
> *"When I was younger."*
> *"Going to baseball games with my family."*
>
> ★ **Has a Complete Thought.** Here is an example of a complete sentence:
> *"When I was younger, I loved going to baseball games with my family."*

A **clause** is a group of words with a subject and predicate. Some clauses are sentences, but others are not. Clauses beginning with **after, until, because,** or **since** do not express a complete thought. These **dependent clauses** cannot stand on their own. The words introducing the clauses show a relationship. When these clauses stand alone, part of the relationship is missing.

For example, *"After I went shopping."* Here, the reader asks what happened *after* you went shopping. The clause does not have a complete thought. It needs to be joined to a main, or independent, clause.

CHECKING YOUR UNDERSTANDING

Check (✔) the examples that are complete sentences.

- ❏ Before I went to bed.
- ❏ They listened to the radio.
- ❏ Since you left.
- ❏ He had eggs yesterday.
- ❏ Because she was hungry.
- ❏ I enjoy your company.

Verbs ending in **ing** cannot be used as the **predicate** (*verb*) of a sentence without a helping verb. For example, *"The girls baking cookies"* is not a sentence. The predicate is incomplete. If you add the helping verb **are,** the fragment becomes a complete sentence: *"The girls **are baking** cookies."*

The best way to correct a sentence fragment is to complete the thought or to supply the missing predicate. Often you can complete the idea or supply the missing predicate by combining the fragment with a neighboring sentence.

For instance, look at the following example:

> *"While I was washing my hands. My family sat down to dinner."*

In this example, "while I was washing my hands" is a **dependent clause.** Although it has a subject and predicate, it does not express a complete thought. The reader wants to know what happened *while* you were washing your hands. You can correct this error by joining this dependent clause to the next sentence: *"While I was washing my hands, my family sat down to dinner."*

RUN-ON SENTENCES

The opposite of a sentence fragment is a run-on sentence. A **run-on sentence** usually occurs when the writer joins several separate sentences together by commas. For example:

> *"Nancy liked the summer, her father preferred the fall."*

CORRECTING RUN-ON SENTENCES

There are several ways to correct run-on sentences. One way is to divide the run-on sentence into two or more separate sentences. A second approach is to turn the run-on sentence into a *compound* or *complex* sentence by adding *conjunctions* or *relative pronouns*. Let's examine each of these approaches for correcting the run-on sentence above:

★ **Create Two or More Separate Sentences.** You can divide the independent clauses of the run-on sentence to create two separate sentences. Each of these new sentences must have its own subject and predicate and express a complete thought:

> *"Nancy liked the summer. Her father preferred the fall."*

★ **Make a Compound Sentence.** You can combine the sentences to make a compound sentence by using a coordinating conjunction such as ***and, or, but*** or ***so***. Remember that a comma must be placed *before* this type of conjunction. Use ***and*** if the two independent clauses are alike; use ***but*** if you want to show how they are different:

> *"Nancy liked the summer, but her father preferred the fall."*

★ **Make a Complex Sentence.** A **complex sentence** has a *dependent clause*. A dependent clause may be introduced by a subordinate conjunction, such as ***when, as, since, although, because,*** or ***while***. Remember that this conjunction shows a link between the two clauses. You must choose the conjunction that best expresses their relationship. Usually no comma is needed when the main clause comes first:

> *"Nancy liked summer although her father preferred the fall."*

> *"Although Nancy liked the summer, her father preferred the fall."*

A second way to make a complex sentence is by introducing the dependent clause *with a special pronoun*, such as ***who, which, that,*** or ***whom***.

> *"Nancy liked summer, which her father didn't like as much as fall."*

COMBINING SENTENCES

You may be asked to rewrite or combine short and choppy sentences on the revising and editing section on the test. Use the same techniques you used to correct run-on sentences to combine short, choppy sentences into longer compound and complex sentences:

> Nancy liked the summer. Her father preferred the fall.

> Nancy liked summer, but her father preferred the fall.

GIVE IT A TRY

Julia is a fourth grader who wrote a composition for her social studies class. Read her composition and think about the corrections and improvements she should make. Then answer the multiple-choice questions that follow.

ELEANOR ROOSEVELT — A GREAT AMERICAN

(1) Eleanor Roosevelt was born on October 17, 1884. (2) When she was 15 years old. (3) In those days, a young lady like Eleanor went to many parties. (4) Eleanor attended most of these parties with her cousin, Franklin Roosevelt. (5) Soon, she and Franklin fell in love. (6) They decided to get married. (7) Franklin's mother asked Eleanor many questions.

(8) Franklin wanted to do something great with his life. (9) He wanted to become President of the United States. (10) Then he caught a disease called polio. (11) The disease left him unable to use his legs. (12) Franklin's mother wanted him to stay at home. (13) Eleanor was determined to have him to continue his political career. (14) And she succeeded! (15) Franklin Roosevelt eventually became America's thirty-seventh President.

(16) Later, the country went to war. (17) Because Franklin was paralyzed, Eleanor became his eyes and ears. (18) She went to many meetings and visited all corners of the country, (19) Sadly, President Roosevelt died just before the war ended. (20) Eleanor went to work in the United Nations. (21) She helped write a declaration promising basic rights to all peoples around the world. (22) Eleanor was a big-hearted person. (23) She was truly a great American.

1. Which of the following is **NOT** a complete sentence?

   A Sentence 1
   B Sentence 2
   C Sentence 4
   D Sentence 5

2. Which sentence could **BEST** be added after sentence 7?

   A Then she agreed to let Franklin marry her.
   B Eleanor's mother had always wanted Eleanor to speak French.
   C Eleanor's mother died when she was very young.
   D Eleanor's father died shortly after her mother died.

3. What is the best way to combine sentences 5 and 6?

   A Soon, she and Franklin fell in love, they decided to get married.
   B Soon, she and Franklin fell in love, since they decided to get married.
   C Soon, she and Franklin fell in love and decided to get married.
   D Soon, she and Franklin fell in love but they decided to get married.

4. Which is the **BEST** way to rewrite the ideas in sentences 12 and 13?

   A Franklin's mother wanted him to stay at home and Eleanor was determined to have him continue his political career.
   B Although Franklin's mother wanted him to stay at home, but Eleanor was determined to have him continue his political career.
   C Franklin's mother wanted him to stay at home or Eleanor was determined to have him continue his political career.
   D Franklin's mother wanted him to stay at home, but Eleanor was determined to have him continue his political career.

5. Which sentence could **BEST** be added after sentence 18?

   A She reported back to Franklin what she saw.
   B She enjoyed cooking for the President.
   C Franklin was President for 12 years.
   D President Roosevelt gave a radio address each week.

CHAPTER 18

USAGE

The revising and editing part of the TAKS will also test your understanding of English usage. Rules of usage govern how to use each part of speech correctly.

NOUNS

A **noun** is a word that names a person, place, or thing.

★ A **proper noun** names a particular person, place or thing. A proper noun always starts with a capital letter: *A*ustin, *M*aple *S*treet, *U*nited *S*tates.

★ Most nouns become plural by adding *s*. To form the plural of nouns ending in *s, z, x, ch,* or *sh,* add *es*. For nouns ending in *y*, change the *y* to *i* and add *es*. A few nouns do not change in the plural.

Singular	Plural	Singular	Plural
hat	hats	story	stories
church	churches	sheep	sheep
brush	brushes	memory	memories

★ Nouns form possessives by adding an apostrophe ' and *s*. A plural noun can show possession by adding the apostrophe after the *s*.

Singular Noun	Plural Noun
These are Jack's books.	This is the teams' clubhouse.

PRONOUNS

A **pronoun** takes the place of a noun used earlier in a speech or writing. The most common pronouns are *I, we, you, he, she, it,* and *they.*

★ It must be clear to the reader what noun the pronoun is replacing. If it is unclear what the pronoun refers to, you should replace the pronoun with the original noun.

★ The pronoun should be the same *gender* (male: **he** or **his** / female: **she** or **her**) and *number* (singular or plural) as the noun it stands for.

★ Pronouns take different forms when they are used to do different jobs in a sentence:

- If the pronoun is used as the *subject* of a sentence use: *I, we, you, he, she, it,* and *they.* For example, "**He** liked to eat candy."

- If the pronoun is used as the object of a sentence or phrase, use an *object pronoun:* **me, us, you, him, her, it,** and **them.** For example, "Rachel loved to eat **pancakes**. She ate **them** almost every day."

SOME TROUBLESOME PRONOUNS

★ *It's* is a contraction for *it is. Its* without an apostrophe shows possession.

- "**It's** time for you to return the bicycle to **its** owner"

★ *There — their — they're*

- *There* is for a place: "*It is over **there**.*"
- *Their* shows possession: "***Their** taxi is waiting.*"
- *They're* is a contraction for *they are*: "***They're** ready to leave.*"

★ *Who, Whose, Who's*

- *Who* is used as the subject of a sentence or clause. "***Who** is that?*"
- *Who's* is a contraction for *who is*: "***Who's** that?*" (Who is that?)
- *Whose* is a possessive referring to ownership: "***Whose** book is that?*"

CHECKING YOUR UNDERSTANDING

Select the correct form of the word to complete the following sentences:

1. (***Its*** / ***It's***) time for us to go home.
2. Are these (***your*** / ***you're***) hat and gloves?
3. (***There*** / ***Their*** / ***They're***) is where the monster lives.
4. It seems that (***your*** / ***you're***) sitting in my chair.

FOR QUESTIONS ON PRONOUNS

(1) It must be clear whom or what the pronoun refers to. If it is unclear, the answer may be to replace the pronoun with the noun it is supposed to refer to.

(2) When answering a question on pronouns, make sure the pronoun "agrees" with the noun it refers to in number and gender. For example, the pronoun must be singular if it replaces a singular noun.

(3) A pronoun must also be in the proper case. If it is the subject of a sentence, make sure it is a subject pronoun. If it is an object, check that it is an object pronoun.

(4) Be sure to choose the correct pronoun for troublesome pronoun groups.

VERBS

Verbs tell us what the subject does or what is being done to the subject in a sentence. They tell us how the subject is, seems, or feels. For example, action verbs like *walk, jump,* and *run* tell what action the subject of a sentence takes.

★ The *tense* of a verb tells us whether the action is in the *past, present* or *future*. Use verb tenses consistently. For example, if a story takes place in the past, all the verbs should usually stay in the past tense.

★ To make the present tense of most verbs in the "third person," add *s* if the subject is singular. Use the plain form of the verb without *s* for plural subjects.

| John *plays* baseball. | John and Susan *play* baseball. |

★ To make the past tense of most verbs, add **ed.** For example: "Dinosaurs once **lived** in this area."

★ Many common verbs take an irregular form in the past tense.

Present Tense	Past Tense	Present Tense	Past Tense
begin	began	come	came
give	gave	get	got

★ Keep verbs in the right tense. If a story takes place in the past, keep all the verbs in the past tense. Change the tense of the verb only if the action moves to the present or future.

Last week, the grumpy sailor *ate* at the old inn. He *had* a meal of fish and *washed* it down with some wine. Then he *went* to sleep in the loft in the stables above the horses. Next week, he *will go* back to work with the new captain of the ship.

SOME TROUBLESOME VERB PAIRS

learn / teach	to **learn** is to receive knowledge: "He **learned** algebra."
	to **teach** is to explain or instruct: "He **taught** the class."
leave / let	to **leave** is to go or depart: "She will **leave** work early."
	to **let** is to permit or allow: "He **let** her use his pencil."

FOR QUESTIONS ON VERBS

(1) When looking at verbs, be sure that the tense of each verb agrees with the action in the sentence. If the action taking place in the sentence is in the past, the verb should be in the past tense. The same goes for present or future actions.

(2) Be sure you have used the correct form of the verb — especially for irregular verbs.

(3) Make sure you have chosen the correct verb from troublesome verb pairs.

ADJECTIVES

An **adjective** describes or modifies a noun. An adjective usually goes before a noun. For example, "The *pretty* girl walked away." The adjective *pretty* is used in this sentence to describe the noun, the *girl*.

★ *A* is used before a consonant. *An* is used before words beginning with a vowel:

- *a* car, *a* book, *a* church, *a* bike
- *an* iceberg, *an* egg, *an* apple

★ Adjectives can be used to compare people, places, or things.

- To say that one thing is superior to another, add *er* to the adjective: "*Jack is taller than Eric.*" This form compares two things.

- To say one thing is the *most* or *best* out of more than two, add *est*: "*Adbul is the tallest boy in the class.*"
"*This is the highest I ever climbed.*"

★ Some adjectives use *more* and *most* for comparisons. For example: "*This is the most delicious apple I ever tasted.*" Never use *more* or *most* with the *er* or *est* forms of the word. Incorrect: "This is the *most* hott*est* day."

★ Remember to use **than,** not **then,** in making comparisons. **Then** refers to a moment in time. "Julie was older **than** Serena."

"Joan went to the store. **Then** she went home."

FOR QUESTIONS ON ADJECTIVES

(1) Questions about adjectives often involve comparisons. To compare two things, add <u>er</u> to the adjective or use <u>more</u> with a longer adjective.

(2) If the thing is the most or best out of more than two, then use the <u>est</u> form or <u>most</u> with a longer adjective.

ADVERBS

Adverbs describe or modify verbs, adjectives, or other adverbs. They are used to add detail to the action of a sentence. For example, "The green car went **quickly** up the large hill." "Quickly" tells us how the car **went.**

★ Many adjectives can be changed into adverbs by adding **ly.** For example, **quick** becomes **quickly,** and **slow** becomes **slowly.**

★ **Good** is an adjective, not an adverb. Use **well** as the adverb, and use **good** as the adjective. "He played **well.**" Incorrect: "He played **good.**"

★ Never use a **double negative** when you write. This sentence is wrong: "He **won't never** succeed at the rate he's moving." Instead, you should write, "He **won't** ever succeed" or "He will **never** succeed."

FOR QUESTIONS ON ADVERBS

(1) In questions involving adverbs, first make sure that an adverb and not an adjective is required. Then be sure to use the adverb.

(2) Be careful not to use double negatives in sentences.

PREPOSITIONS

A **preposition** links a *noun* or *pronoun* to another word or phrase in the sentence: "She sat *at* the table." Some common prepositions are: *of, at, on, about,* and *behind.*

★ If the object of the preposition is a pronoun, it must be an **object pronoun.** For example: "Jim gave it to *me.*"

> **FOR QUESTIONS ON PREPOSITIONS**
> (1) Many questions on prepositions test your use of pronouns. If a pronoun is an object of a preposition, be sure it is an object pronoun.

SUBJECT-VERB AGREEMENT

A very common usage error is in *subject / verb agreement.* The subject and verb (*predicate*) of the sentence must agree in number.

★ A **singular subject** refers to one person, place or thing. If the subject of a sentence is singular, you must use a verb in its **singular form.**

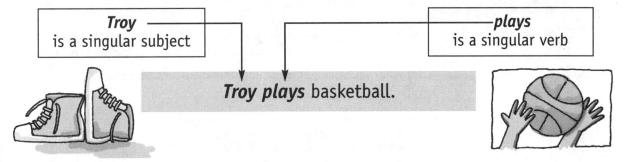

Troy is a singular subject

plays is a singular verb

Troy plays basketball.

★ A **plural subject** consists of more than one person, place, or thing. The subject may be a plural noun (*children*) or a compound subject (*Jim and Jack*). If the subject of a sentence is plural, the verb must be in its plural form.

Jack *likes* to drink water.
John and Jack *like* to drink water.
The children *like* to drink water.

★ Remember that interrupting words and phrases do not change the subject from singular to plural or from plural to singular. To identify the correct subject, it sometimes helps to cross out all the modifiers and phrases that come between the subject and verb.

> The **man** with three sisters *is* sitting on the couch.

- In this example, the subject remains singular — "man." Although he has three sisters, this information is in a prepositional phrase describing the man. It does not change the subject from singular to plural. A singular verb is needed.

FOR QUESTIONS ON SUBJECT–VERB AGREEMENT

(1) To check for subject–verb agreement, first identify the subject and verb of the sentence. You may want to cross out all interrupting words and phrases, especially prepositional phrases that may confuse you.

(2) If the subject is plural, make sure the verb is also in plural form. If the subject is singular, use a verb in singular form.

GIVE IT A TRY

Maria is a fourth grader who wrote a brief story for her English class. Read her story and think about the corrections and improvements she should make. Then answer the multiple-choice questions that follow.

A TALL TALE: TIGER JONES

(1) Once upon a time, there were small boy named Tiger Jones. (2) Tiger wasn't no ordinary boy. (3) When he were three years old, he could wrestle with a tiger. (4) At the age of six, he could run fastest than a cheetah. (5) When he grows older, Tiger wanted to see the world. (6) He hopped from mountain top to mountain top. (7) When he saw some farmers having trouble from the lack of rain, Tiger Jones dug a huge ditch. (8) It filled with water and became the Mississippi River.

1. What change, if any, should be made in sentence 1?
   - A Change *upon* to *up on*
   - B Change *were* to *was*
   - C Change *small* to *smal*
   - D Make no change

2. What change, if any, should be made in sentence 2?
   - A Change *wasn't* to *was*
   - B Change *wasn't* to *were*
   - C Change *no* to *none*
   - D Make no change

3. What change, if any, should be made in sentence 3?
   - A Change *he* to *she*
   - B Change *were* to *was*
   - C Change *could* to *can*
   - D Make no change

4. What change, if any, should be made in sentence 4?
   - A Change *could* to *can*
   - B Change *fastest* to *faster*
   - C Change *than* to *then*
   - D Make no change

5. What change, if any, should be made in sentence 5?
   - A Change *he* to *she*
   - B Change *grows* to *grew*
   - C Change *older* to *oldest*
   - D Make no change

6. What word could be used in place of *It* in sentence 8?
   - A The ditch
   - B Tiger Jones
   - C The farmers
   - D The rain

CHAPTER 19

MECHANICS

A final area of writing conventions tested on the **TAKS Grade 4 in Writing** is mechanics — the rules of spelling, capitalization, and punctuation.

SPELLING

At one time, there were no rules for spelling. People spelled each word in their own way. Today, there is common agreement about the spelling of most words. Here are some general rules that will help you to spell correctly.

★ **Changing final *y* to *i*.** When a noun ends in *y* after a consonant, change the *y* to *i* and add *es* to make it plural. For example:

> *story* ➜ *stories*   *city* ➜ *cities*   *memory* ➜ *memories*

★ **Dropping the final *e*.** When a noun ends in a consonant plus an *e*, drop the final *e* before adding *ing*. For example:

> *hide* ➜ *hiding*   *love* ➜ *loving*   *make* ➜ *making*

★ **Words with *ei* and *ie*.** In general, use *i* before *e*, except after *c*, or when sounding like *ay*, as in **neighbor** or **weigh**. Some words that follow this rule include **piece, chief, believe,** and **receive**. However, there are some exceptions to the rule, such as **weird** and **seize**.

★ **Plural of nouns ending with *f*.** If a noun ends in *f*, change the *f* to *v* and then add *es* to make it plural. For example:

> *wolf* ➜ *wolves*   *shelf* ➜ *shelves*   *elf* ➜ *elves*

★ **Words with *ght*.** Some words end with *ght* to make the sound *t*. Do not confuse their spelling — ***eight, night, height,*** and ***weight.***

★ **Silent *e*.** Many English words end in a silent *e*, especially when the sound of the preceding vowel is "long" (*says its name*): flam*e*, estimat*e*, irritat*e*, despit*e*, compromis*e*.

★ **Words with *ph*.** Words with *ph* make an *f* sound

| photogra*ph*y | biogra*ph*y | trium*ph* |

★ **Spelling Hot Spots.** When you misspell a word or learn a new word, you should look carefully at the word. Often there is a "hot spot" that makes the word difficult to spell. Focus on the "hot spot." Make a circle around it. Then write the word several times from memory. Keep a list of words you have difficulty spelling. Practice spelling them.

CHECKING YOUR UNDERSTANDING

*Circle the "hot spot" in each of the following words.
The first word has been done for you*

T(ues)day	weather	balloon	swimming
across	coming	pleasant	address
their	friend	afraid	separate
receive	there	February	Wednesday

CAPITALIZATION

Capitalization tells us when something is important. It could be important because it is the beginning of a sentence or simply an important word. Either way, capitalization makes us sit up and take notice.

★ A proper noun should always begin with a capital letter.

- *Days, months, streets, cities,* and *countries* are all proper nouns that should begin with a capital letter. *Monday, July, Thanksgiving, Austin, Mexico.*
- People's names are always capitalized: **Jack, Margaret Smith**
- Personal titles followed by a name are capitalized: **President Bush, Mrs. Lincoln, Dr. Salk, Captain Jones**
- Family members followed by the person's name are capitalized: **Uncle Jim, Aunt Sarah, Cousin Mary**

★ Always begin a sentence with a capital letter and always capitalize the pronoun *I*.

★ **Titles.** Capitalize the first word and all the main words of *book titles* (**War and Peace**), newspapers (**Austin Statesman**), *magazines* (**Newsweek**), *movies, plays, poems,* and *songs.* Do not capitalize prepositions, articles (**the, a**) or conjunctions (**and, but,** and **or**) in titles.

CHECKING YOUR UNDERSTANDING

Correct the following paragraph by capitalizing as needed.

for most of his childhood, timothy had yearned for the freedom of a life at sea. at the age of 13, he ran away from home and joined a ship's crew at portsmouth, england. His first voyage took him to canada, the united states, south america, australia, hong kong, and india. two years later, timothy finally returned to england. he later wrote down the story of his adventures in his book, my life at sea.

PUNCTUATION

Punctuation marks are like street signs. They tell us when to go, pause, or stop.

★ Use commas to separate the day of the month from the year in a date, and to separate the date from the rest of the sentence. For example: *On July 20, 1969, the United States landed a man on the moon.*

- ★ Use **commas** to separate the name of a city from the place in which it is located. For example: *Albany, New York; Boston, Massachusetts*
- ★ Use **commas** between words in a series: *apples, oranges, and grapes*
- ★ Use **commas** to set off phrases: *Robert, a quiet man, was very excited.*
- ★ Use **commas** before the conjunctions **and, or,** and **but** in compound sentences: *He went to the bank, and she drove to school.*
- ★ Use **commas** and **quotation marks** to show direct speech. If the sentence ends with the quotation, put quotation marks outside the end of the sentence: *She said, "I went to the movies."*
- ★ **End marks** indicate the end of a sentence:
  - **Periods** are used to end declaratory sentences and for some commands, as well as abbreviations: *Ms. Jones was delighted.*
  - **Question marks** are used to end questions: *What did you say?*
  - **Exclamation marks** end strong expressions of emotion and some commands: *Get out of my house!*
- ★ **Apostrophes** are used to show possession or in contractions to show that letters are missing from a word:
  - He's wearing *Tom's hat*
  - *He can't do that.*

CHECKING YOUR UNDERSTANDING

Insert the correct punctuation in the following paragraph:

It was late at night on October 13 ☐ 1995 ☐ Everything was quiet in the house ☐ Suddenly we heard a crash ☐ A large number of people rushed out of their homes to see what was going on ☐ ☐ Is anyone hurt ☐ ☐ our neighbor asked ☐ ☐ It looks as if there was an earthquake ☐ ☐ my mother answered ☐

GIVE IT A TRY

Kyle is a fourth grader who wrote a report for his science class. Read part of his report and think about the corrections and improvements he should make. Then answer the multiple-choice questions that follow.

THE STUDY OF ANIMALS

(1) Scientists who study diferent life forms are known as biologists. (2) Biologists have identified too main forms of animals. (3) Invertebrates are animals without backbones! (4) Sponges, clams and insects, are invertebrates. (5) The second kind of animals are vertebrates. (6) Vertebrates have backbones. (7) Snakes, fish and human beings are vertebrates.

---

1 What change, if any, should be made in sentence 1?

  A Change *biologist* to *Biologist*
  B Add a comma after *scientists*
  C Change *diferent* to *different*
  D Make no change

2 What change, if any, should be made in sentence 2?

  A Change *have* to *halve*
  B Change *too* to *two*
  C Change *main* to *mane*
  D Make no change

3 What change, if any, should be made in sentence 3?

  A Add a comma after *animals*
  B Change the exclamation mark to a question mark
  C Change the exclamation mark to a period
  D Make no change

4 What change, if any, should be made in sentence 4?

  A Change *sponges* to *spunges*
  B Remove the comma after *insects*
  C Change *invertebrate* to *Invertebrates*
  D Make no change

UNIT 6: A FINAL PRACTICE WRITING TEST

In this final section, you will have the opportunity to practice your skills to see how much you have learned. This practice test is designed to be just like the actual **TAKS Grade 4 in Writing.**

The test has two parts. The first part consists of a writing prompt. You will have the freedom to respond to the writing prompt with any form of writing you choose. However, your writing should show the qualities of *focus and coherence, organization,* the *development of ideas,* and *voice,* and follow the *standard conventions of written English.* To write your composition on the TAKS, follow the same steps you take in all your writing. Begin by *thinking about* what you are going to write. Take time to create an outline or other *prewriting plan* for your composition. Then write your *first draft* and *revise and edit* what you have written. Finally, *write* and *proofread* your final draft.

The second part of the test has four student compositions, followed by multiple-choice questions. On each of these compositions, you must do some revising and editing. The peer editing questions show the writing convention being tested. This test will help you and your teacher to identify any kinds of questions you may need additional practice in answering. If you should finish early, use the time to check over your work.

Good luck on this practice test!

Chapter 20

A PRACTICE TAKS GRADE 4 IN WRITING

PART 1: THE WRITING PROMPT

On a separate sheet of paper, write a composition addressing the following writing prompt.

> **Write a composition about your favorite time of the year.**

The information in the box below will help you remember what you should think about when you write your composition.

REMEMBER — YOU SHOULD

- ❏ write about your favorite time of the year
- ❏ make sure that each sentence you write helps the reader understand your composition
- ❏ write about your ideas in detail so that the reader really understands what you are saying
- ❏ try to use correct spelling, capitalization, punctuation, grammar and sentences

PART 2:
THE REVISING AND EDITING SECTION

Marsha is in the fourth grade. Her teacher asked each student to write about an exciting game. Marsha chose to write about a basketball game. This is a draft of her paper. Marsha wants you to help her revise and edit it. Read Marsha's paper and think about changes you would make to help her improve it. Then answer the questions that follow.

AN EXCITING GAME

(1) Today, I had a basketball game. (2) I am the taller member of our team. (3) My father took me to the local gym. (4) Where I met my teammates.

(5) We were playing a team called the Rockets. (6) It looked as if most of the players on the Rockets could dribble or shoot very good. (7) Then I saw Katy, an enormous player. (8) Katy was taller then any other fourth grader. (9) She was so large I thought the basketball court might crack when she walked on it.

(10) The referee blew the whistle, the game started. (11) I had to jump against Katy. (12) Obviously, the other team got the ball. (13) Rachel is the fastest runner on our team. (14) The guard on the other team dribbled the ball down the court. (15) We stole the ball and scored our first basket?

(16) The rest of the game was just as exciting. (17) Katy got most of the rebounds, but she didn't make many baskets. (18) Our team had shorter players, but we won the game!

1 What change, if any, should be made in sentence 2?

    A Change *am* to *are*
    B Change *the* to *a*
    C Change *taller* to *tallest*
    D Make no change

Usage

2 What is the **BEST** way to combine sentences 3 and 4?

A My father took me to the local gym, and where I met my teammates.

B My father took me to the local gym, where I met my teammates.

C My father took me to the local gym, which I met my teammates.

D Although my father took me to the local gym where I met my teammates

Sentence Construction

3 What change, if any, should be made in sentence 6?

A Change *most* to *more*
B Change *could* to *couldn't*
C Change *good* to *well*
D Make no change

Usage

4 What change, if any, should be made in sentence 8?

A Change *was* to *wasn't*
B Change *taller* to *tallest*
C Change *then* to *than*
D Make no change

Usage

5 What is the **BEST** way to revise sentence 10?

A The referee blew the whistle but the game started.
B Although the referee blew the whistle the game started.
C Once the referee blew the whistle, the game started.
D The referee blew the whistle, however the game started.

Sentence Construction

6 Which sentence does **NOT** belong in the third paragraph (sentences 10 — 15)?

A Sentence 11
B Sentence 12
C Sentence 13
D Sentence 14

Organization

7 What change, if any, should be made in sentence 15?

A Change *stole* to *steel*
B Add a comma after *ball*
C Change the question mark after *basket* to a period
D Make no change

Mechanics

Thomas is a fourth grader. He wrote a report for his science class to tell about our solar system. Read his report and think about the corrections and improvements Thomas should make. Then answer the questions that follow.

THE STORY OF OUR SOLAR SYSTEM

(1) For thousands of years, people have watchd the sky and looked at the stars. (2) Ancient peoples believed they saw the shapes of gods and goddesses in the sky. (3) Today, we call these groups of stars constellations.

(4) The ancient peoples of Egypt and Greece also observed the stars for another reason. (5) They used them to guide their ships. (6) They kept records of the movement of the stars and planets. (7) They believed the planets made curling patterns around the earth. (8) At times the planets seemed to move forwards, while at other times the planets seemed to move backwards.

(9) In the 1400s, a polish astronomer named Nicholas Copernicus came up with a new idea. (10) Until that time, everyone thought the planets moved around the earth. (11) Copernicus said that the planets, including the earth, moved around the sun. (12) At first, most people resisted this idea, they could not imagine that the earth was not the center of the universe. (13) Authorities threatened to punish anyone who spread the ideas of Copernicus.

(14) The invention of the telescope helped scientists prove that Copernicus was right. (15) Gradually, everyone came to accept the Copernican view of our solar system. (16) Scientists learned the importance of careful observation, leading to a "scientific revolution."

(17) Today, scientists still study the skies. (18) Spacecraft have landed on Venus and Mars. (19) Scientists have not used the full potential of the atom. (20) Someday, manned flights may land on these planets. (21) There is still much we do not know. (22) About the planets and the stars.

8 What change, if any, should be made in sentence 1?

A Change *thousands* to *thousand*
B Change *watchd* to *watched*
C Change *looked* to *lookt*
D Make no change *Mechanics*

9 What change, if any, should be made in sentence 4?

A Change *ancient* to *Ancient*
B Add a comma after *Greece*
C Change the period after *reason* to a question mark.
D Make no change *Mechanics*

10 The meaning of sentence 5 can be improved by changing *them* to —

A this reason
B these ancient peoples
C the stars
D the seas *Usage*

11 What change, if any, should be made in sentence 9?

A Change *polish* to *Polish*
B Change *astronomer* to *Astronomer*
C Change *Nicholas Copernicus* to *nicholas copericus*
D Make no change *Mechanics*

12 What is the **BEST** way to rewrite the ideas in sentence 12?

A At first, most people resisted this idea because they could not imagine that the earth was not the center of the universe.
B At first, most people resisted this idea. Because they could not imagine that the earth was not the center of the universe.
C At first, because most people resisted this idea. They could not imagine that the earth was not the center of the universe.
D At first, most people resisted this idea? They could not imagine that the earth was not the center of the universe.

Sentence Construction

13 Which sentence does **NOT** belong in this paper?

A Sentence 3
B Sentence 4
C Sentence 18
D Sentence 19 *Organization*

14 Which of the following is **NOT** a complete sentence?

A Sentence 7
B Sentence 8
C Sentence 21
D Sentence 22 *Sentence Construction*

Manuel is in the fourth grade. His teacher asked each student to write a composition about someone they know. Manuel wrote about his sister, Juanita. This is a draft of his paper. Manuel wants you to help him revise and edit it. Read Manuel's paper and think about changes you would make to help him improve it. Then answer the questions that follow.

MY SISTER, JUANITA

(1) Have you ever lived with someone for seven years and still not really known that person good? (2) I have lived in the same house as my younger sister, Juanita, since I was three years old. (3) Even so, sometimes I just don't understand her.

(4) Juanitas' personality is very different from mine. (5) For example, she has a bad temper. (6) She will get very angry if I try to tell her what to do. (7) I don't like it when other people tell me what to do, either. (8) I don't scream at them.

(9) However, there are some important similarities between us. (10) When we are with friends. (11) We both feel very happy. (12) We also both likes talking, although Juanita is more talkative than I am. (13) Like me, Juanita can find humor in almost anything. (14) When Dad tells his silly jokes, we both pretend they are funny and start to laugh, even though they are not. (15) Then we look each other in the eye and laugh even harder.

(16) My younger sister is annoyed at times, but she is also a loving and caring sister. (17) I may not always understand her, but I am glad to have her as my sister and friend.

15 What change, if any, should be made in sentence 1?

    A Change *Have* to *Are*
    B Change *known* to *know*
    C Change *good* to *well*
    D Make no change

Usage

16 What change, if any, should be made in sentence 4?

A Change **Juanitas'** to **Juanita's**
B Change **different** to **differently**
C Change the period after **mine** to a question mark
D Make no change *Mechanics*

17 What sentence could **BEST** be added after sentence 6?

A She likes pizza while I prefer tacos.
B We both play basketball.
C She still plays with dolls.
D She yells and locks herself in her room. *Organization*

18 What is the **BEST** way to combine sentences 7 and 8?

A I don't like it when other people tell me what to do, either, I don't scream at them.
B I don't like it when other people tell me what to do, either and I don't scream at them.
C I don't like it when other people tell me what to do, either, but I don't scream at them.
D I don't like it when other people tell me what to do, and either I don't scream at them. *Sentence Construction*

19 Which of the following is **NOT** a complete sentence?

A Sentence 3
B Sentence 5
C Sentence 10
D Sentence 13 *Sentence Construction*

20 What change, if any, should be made in sentence 12?

A Change **likes** to **like**
B Change **than** to **then**
C Change **I** to **me**
D Make no change *Usage*

21 What change, if any, should be made to sentence 13?

A Change **find** to **fine**
B Change **humor** to **Humor**
C Change the period after **anything** to a question mark
D Make no change *Mechanics*

Angelina is a fourth grader. She wrote this report for her social studies class to tell about the travels of Cabeza de Vaca. Read her report and think about the corrections and improvements Angelina should make. Then answer the questions that follow.

THE TRAVELS OF CABEZA DE VACA

(1) Álvar Núñez Cabeza de Vaca was born in 1490 into a family of spanish nobility. (2) His ancestors had been warriors for centuries. (3) In 1528, he sailed with 300 men from Cuba to Florida in search of gold. (4) The men wandered the land for six months. (5) Not finding any gold. (6) All they found were hostile Native Americans, malaria and dysentery. (7) When they returned to the coast, there ships were gone. (8) The men built large rafts to float along the coast. (9) About 80 of them finally landed on Galveston Island in November 1528.

(10) Cabeza de Vaca now took command. (11) Local Native Americans gave the men food. (12) Unfortunately, some of the Native Americans became ill. (13) They blamed Cabeza de Vaca and his men. (14) Cabeza de Vaca and his men were enslaved by the Native Americans. (15) Only Cabeza de Vaca and three others survived.

(16) After six years in captivity. (17) The four men escaped. (18) They walked over 2,000 miles to Mexico. (19) They finally reached Mexico City in 1536. (20) It was here that Cabeza de Vaca later wrote about his travels. (21) He and his men was the first Europeans to journey through what is now known as Texas. (22) His writings are the oldest written history of the Native Americans of this region.

22 What change, if any, should be made in sentence 1?

A Change *into* to *from*
B Change *spanish* to *Spanish*
C Change the period after *nobility* to a question mark
D Make no change   *Mechanics*

23 What is the **BEST** way to rewrite the ideas in sentences 4 and 5?

A The men wandered the land for six months, and not finding any gold.
B The men wandered the land for six months, but they did not find any gold.
C The men wandered the land for six months, but not finding any gold.
D The men wandered the land for six months, which did not find any gold.   *Sentence Construction*

24 What change, if any, should be made in sentence 7?

A Change *returned* to *returns*
B Remove the comma after *coast*
C Change *there* to *their*
D Make no change   *Usage*

25 What change, if any, should be made in sentence 9?

A Add a comma after *80*
B Add a comma after *Island*
C Add a comma after *November*
D Make no change   *Mechanics*

26 Which of the following is **NOT** a complete sentence?

A Sentence 10
B Sentence 13
C Sentence 16
D Sentence 19   *Sentence Construction*

27 Which sentence could **BEST** be added after sentence 18?

A Mexico achieved its independence in 1821.
B About 300 years later, Stephen Austin started a colony in the same area.
C On their way, they saw herds of buffalo and many different Native American tribes.
D Spanish soldiers had conquered the Aztecs in 1521.

Organization

28 What change, if any, should be made in sentence 21?

A Change *his* to *their*
B Change *was* to *were*
C Change *through* to *thru*
D Make no change   *Usage*